Finger Puppet Mania!

Finger

Karen Hartigan Whiting

Puppet

IA!

Illustrated by Ed Letwinko

Published by Concordia Publishing House
3558 S. Jefferson Avenue, St. Louis, MO 63118-3968
Manufactured in the United States of America

1 2 3 4 5 6 7 8 9 10 08 07 06 05 04 03 02 01 00 99

To my daughter,
Rebecca-Love Whiting,
my first audience,
and the one who started me in puppetry.

Contents

Introduction

Puppets make ideal teaching tools. A puppet transforms a teacher into an entertaining storyteller while the puppet becomes an appealing part of the lesson.

Assemble these simple, movable-mouth finger puppets with cutting, sewing, or gluing. Made from felt, trims, and moving or painted eyes, the cost is minimal and the small puppets store flat.

Movable-mouth finger puppets make versatile teaching tools. Each animal puppet can be used to introduce values related to characteristics of the animal or Bible events involving the animal. A puppet can pop out at any time to remind children of rules or to help teach a Bible verse. Adopt a special puppet pet to assist in teaching a unit.

Special character puppets awaken imaginations and provide a method of introducing biblical imagery to children. For example, a candle puppet can be used to introduce the concept of Jesus as the Light of the world.

Use your imagination to create your own finger puppet mania!

Making Finger Puppets

Materials to Stock and Stack

- Felt scraps, assorted colors
- Craft foam, assorted colors (for eyes, teeth, nostrils)
- Movable craft eyes (purchased at craft stores)
- Fabric glue (a type of tacky glue works best)
- Fabric paint, white and assorted colors (or fabric markers)
- Sewing machine and thread (or needle and thread)

Easy-to-Follow Directions

Except where specifically noted, follow these step-by-step directions when assembling each finger puppet.

1. Using the reproducible patterns provided, place the patterns on top of a piece of felt, using suggested or desired colors. (Remember that animals do not have to be true to nature's colors!) Then cut out each piece.
2. Assemble the pieces placing wrong sides of felt together.
3. Match points A and B. Sew or glue the pieces together from A to B. This will form the bottom of the mouth.
4. Match points C and D. Sew or glue from C to D. This will form the top of the mouth and the head.
5. Fold the long, oval piece in half, with the head on top. Two pockets will be formed. Insert your fingers into the upper pocket and your thumb into the lower pocket. Lower and raise your thumb to work the puppet's mouth.
6. Add the eyes, tongue, and nose or nostrils. Use fabric paint or craft foam to make teeth and other features. If small children will be using the puppets, paint the eyes rather than gluing on small objects that can be swallowed. For hair, attach yarn or a rectangle of felt that has been cut into thin strips, leaving one end uncut for attaching.
7. (Optional) Wear these finger puppets in a pocket, with the head sticking out!
8. (Optional) Covering your hand with a black glove (or one that matches the puppet) will help the animal appear real. Cut off the fingertips of the glove for easier gripping. To make a quick glove, cut off one leg of a pair of tights at the knee. In the toe area, cut one hole for your thumb, and a large hole for your fingers.

9. (Optional) To add a body, cut a flat body-front out of felt and sew it to the lower edge of the puppet's neck.
10. (Optional) Attach a long piece of felt to the back of the head to make a tail that swings down. Or make a tail with a pipe cleaner, shaping it to stick up in the air. Attach invisible thread to the tail and pull it with your free hand to make the tail wiggle!
11. If a tighter thumb opening is desired, sew the outer sides of the lower jaw together, leaving an opening for your thumb. Be sure to fit it with pins first to make sure it is the right size. Or make a thumb grip by gluing a ½-inch by 1-inch strip of craft foam in the puppet's jaws. Place the grip where your thumb can pull against it.

Extra Hands for Helping
Teachers may want to make puppets themselves as a summer project or seek help from various sources:

- Senior members of the church
- Parents
- Teenagers, especially those who might have learned to sew
- Tailors or seamstresses from your local cleaners
- Teacher's aides

Or put a notice in the church bulletin or newsletter inviting assistance from people who enjoy sewing and are willing to volunteer. If your church has a puppet ministry, solicit help from members of the group.

Manipulating Finger Puppets

Movements that Bring Puppets to Life

Puppetry is a performing art where the puppeteer manipulates the puppet to create drama. With finger puppets, the audience imagines the puppet's body movements by watching the movement of the head. For example, when the head of the puppet bobs up and down, the puppet appears to be jumping. The movement brings the puppet to life.

In puppetry, three parts of your body are used to make puppets appear real: the arm, the wrist, and the fingers.

The Arm

The arm moves the puppet's body making it appear to jump, walk, crawl, hop, etc. Movements can be slow or fast, side-to-side, or up-and-down. Your arm can move smoothly or with a jerk.

Each movement produces a different effect:

- A backwards jerk makes the puppet appear surprised or fearful.
- A slow movement forward, hanging over the edge of the stage, makes the puppet appear curious or cautious.
- A fast, choppy, side-to-side movement of the arm makes the puppet appear to run.
- Moving the arm in an up-and-down, circular motion produces a hop.
- A slow, circular motion that increases in speed lets the puppet look dizzy.
- Holding the arm at an angle slightly forward, and moving it slowly, makes the puppet look old.
- A sweeping, side-to-side motion makes the puppet appear to fly or glide.
- Holding the arm in a horizontal position makes the puppet appear to crawl.

Practice making your arm produce various movements and note how each one makes the puppet appear to move.

The most realistic way to bring a puppet into view is to let the puppet walk or hop onto the stage, using a side-to-side movement for walking, and an up-and-down movement to produce a hop. Have the puppet appear from below the stage as though climbing stairs or a hill. The puppet will appear to come from a different location and return to the same place after performing.

Once onstage, keep the puppet at one height so it will not appear to get taller or smaller. To leave the stage, turn the puppet around and let it walk or hop out of sight, descending the stairs or hill.

The Wrist

The wrist changes the direction the puppet is facing, thus changing the focus of the puppet's eyes. Focus is extremely important in puppetry. If the puppet can appear to be looking at the audience, the audience will pay attention. If, instead, the puppet is looking toward the ceiling (unless you want the children to look for something on the ceiling), the children will be distracted and lose interest in the puppet.

With a bend of the wrist, the puppet can look up, down, sideways, or circle around as if dizzy. Movements done at varying speeds, from slow to fast and smooth to jerky, produce effects that give the puppet emotions and personality.

Experiment using movements of your wrist to change the puppet's focus. This will also give the puppet more personality.

- An animal moving slowly with its head hanging down will appear to be sad.
- A puppet that peeks out, then hides its head, will appear shy.
- A puppet that walks onstage, glances around, then stops to stare, will appear to be interested in something. This causes the audience to look at what the puppet sees. Children will follow the puppet's eyes for clues as to what might occur next.

- A puppet that looks below the back of the stage, or behind another puppet's head, will cause children to anticipate that something unexpected is going to happen.
- A puppet that slowly turns its head, then quickly jerks it back to look at a child, will encourage the audience to try to discover what the puppet sees! Those watching will be ready to listen to find out what the puppet knows.
- Try giving a different personality to your puppets so each will appear more lifelike. Here are some wrist exercises to try:
    - Shake your wrist for no or to make puppet appear uncooperative.
    - Move your wrist up and down for yes or to make puppet appear excited.
    - Slowly bend your wrist down and back up to take a bow.
    - Try a puppet sneeze. Move your wrist back, with the puppet's mouth slightly open. Move the puppet forward to its original position and repeat. Then open the puppet's mouth wider, bend your wrist farther back, and jerk the puppet forward and down.
    - Let a puppet look into an open Bible. Move your wrist slowly left-to-right so the puppet appears to be reading. Pivot back to the left when a puppet reaches the end of each line. Stop and bend your wrist lower to make the puppet appear to be studying the words.

The Fingers

Since these are finger puppets, your fingers do the talking! Keep your fingers still and move only your thumb up and down when making the animal talk. Moving your fingers will hide the eyes of the puppet and move them out of view of the audience. In puppetry, this is called "flipping the lid."

Move the puppet's mouth once for each syllable and close it when not talking. To talk fast, close the mouth on every other syllable. Synchronize opening and closing the mouth with the words as they are spoken. Opening the mouth too late will make it look like the puppet is eating the words.

To practice moving the jaw down, hold the top of the puppet against the side of a table. Only the lower jaw will be able to move down because the table will prevent any upper movement. This will force you to correctly open the mouth with the downward movement of your thumb.

Talking Exercises for Practice

- Recite the ABCs.
- Sing some simple songs.
- Create dialogue between two puppets, perhaps performing easy two-line jokes. When one puppet talks to another, have the puppets look at each other. Make sure the puppets also look at the audience, especially when laughing or responding to the other puppet's comments.

Combining the Movements

All three of the body parts (arm, wrist, and fingers) move together to bring the puppet to life. Practice combining movements for greater effectiveness. For example, use your wrist and arms to create snake-like wiggling and use your fingers to open the puppet's mouth for a yawn.

Puppets imitate reality. Observe how people move and talk, then imitate the movements with the puppet. Observe real animals and imitate those movements as well.

Staging Ideas

Hints for Good Puppetry

1. Practice in front of a mirror to see what the audience sees!
2. Try different voices for different characters.
3. For young puppeteers, make an audiotape of the voices so they can lip-sync with the puppets. This allows the children to concentrate on puppetry skills rather than speaking the words.
4. Learn more about the real animal counterpart of your puppet. Working facts and characteristics into your lesson will help the puppet appear more lifelike. The puppet pages in this book include fun facts and suggestions for Bible applications to help you get started!

Putting Puppets in the Spotlight

Without a stage, children will certainly use their imagination and enjoy the puppets. You may, however, want to use a stage for performances. Here are some simple ideas for making stages for finger puppets.

1. **Lunch box stage**

A plastic lunch box is great for storing puppets. To make it into a stage, open the lunch box and stand it on its side. Place the box on a desk and have the puppets perform from behind. If desired, decorate the lunch box as a puppet house with contact paper and markers.

2. **Walk-around stage**

Cut the sides of an empty box to a 4-inch height all around. Cut a large oval in the bottom of the box. Staple a string that has been cut long enough to go around your neck to each end of the box. Make sure the string is long enough to hold the box around your neck at the height you want to hold the stage for performing. Decorate the box with lace, fabric, or contact paper. Place the strap around your neck, put the puppets on your fingers, and insert your hands through the oval opening to perform.

If you want to use more than two puppets during the show, simply screw small hooks inside the box, add loops to the puppets, and hang the extra puppets on the hooks. Just remember where each puppet is hanging so you can make quick changes without looking!

3. **Sheet or blanket stage**

Secure a sturdy string across a doorway. Hang a sheet or blanket over the string to form a stage. Place the sheet high enough for the puppeteer to stand and hold the puppet up and over the top. In standing, the puppeteer can move back and forth, making it easy to move the puppet across the stage.

4. **Folding-board stage**

A folding cardboard cutting board, purchased from a sewing supply store, or a folding-board for a science display, purchased from a school supply store, can be used to make a puppet stage. Cover the folding-board with contact paper or fabric. Large boards can be cut smaller or a window can be cut to create a puppet stage area. This window area is called a *proscenium*. The folding-board stage can be placed on a table or on the floor.

Puppets can perform above the top of the board or be shown through the opening of the window.

Make a crossbar to keep the board open and stabilize it, reaching across the top, from one side to the other. Open the folding-board to the desired width. Cut a piece of 2-inch wide heavy cardboard or lightweight wood to a length two inches longer than the distance from one side of the stage to the other, a few inches back from the hinge or fold in the cardboard. Cut 2-inch slits in the crossbar, one inch in from each end. Cut slits in the top of the stage at the points measured. Slide the crossbar into the slits. If you are using a proscenium, scenery or a curtain can be hung on the crossbar.

Teaching with Puppets

Using Puppets with Children

Puppets are versatile and grab attention, so use them to captivate your audience. Creative ideas include:

- Using puppets to introduce a Bible lesson
- Using a puppet to repeat a Bible verse, or letting the puppet get confused so the children can help it say the verse correctly
- Using puppets to help tell a Bible story (such as an animal on Noah's ark, a donkey Jesus rode into Jerusalem on Palm Sunday, or a pig that was fed by the prodigal son)
- Using a puppet to help a shy child feel welcome
- Using a puppet to introduce a new child
- Using a puppet to give a hug or kiss to a child
- Using a puppet to lead singing
- Using a puppet to talk about an upcoming event in order to help children remember it, get excited about it, and know the necessary information
- Using a puppet to reinforce correct behavior by having it compliment desired behavior
- Using a puppet to introduce special guests or programs

Adding Interesting Facts to the Lessons

Each animal or special character featured as a puppet has unique qualities. Use each particular puppet to explain how its unique characteristics can illustrate a Bible truth. Use the following suggestions or think of your own new ideas.

- Use an oyster puppet to tell how adversity is turned into beauty as an irritating grain of sand is turned into a pearl.
- Use a candle puppet to explain how a light helps others find their way.
- Use an elephant puppet to give hints for remembering and memorizing Bible verses.
- Use a Bible puppet to introduce a Bible verse or explain its meaning.
- Use a hand puppet to lead a discussion on ways to help others.

Wordless Puppetry

Puppets can be used to pantomime familiar situations, thus helping children better understand an illustration. For example, one puppet can steal from another to illustrate sin. Because the puppet cannot actually commit sin or receive forgiveness, provide a link between the puppet's situation and the life of God's children as they live out their faith through the power of the Holy Spirit.

Use the following scenarios for puppets to pantomime or think of your own to add to the list.

- A puppet tries to cheer up another puppet who is sad by giving it something. The sad puppet does not cheer up until it receives either a heart or a hug. This illustrates a deeper need for love than for material things. Talk about our deep need for God's love and the saving forgiveness that is ours through the death and resurrection of Jesus.
- One puppet hurts another and leaves. A third puppet helps the hurt puppet, illustrating mercy and love. Use the first two puppets to teach the words "I'm sorry" and "I forgive you," reminding the children these are words for them, not the puppets, to use when they have hurt someone else. Invite the children to add, "I forgive you for Jesus' sake."
- One puppet howls or hums a song. Another puppet tries to stop the one who is singing. The singing puppet points to a sign printed with the Bible verse "Make a joyful noise." Both puppets begin to sing. Talk about ways God's children praise Him.
- A puppet gives money away, contributing to a worthy cause. A second puppet brings money but does not want to give it away. Use this scenario to talk about selfishness and sharing with others what God has given us.

Other Hints on Using Puppets

There are limits to consider when using puppets, especially since puppets are not real. Differentiating between fact and fantasy is difficult for children, especially the very young. Be careful not to confuse fantasy with reality when using puppets.

Be sure that the puppets do not express faith as if they had souls or were capable of believing. Puppets can be used to discuss faith concepts or pantomime a situation,. but help the children understand that the puppet cannot actually sin or be saved by the death and resurrection of Jesus. The puppet is acting out a situation to which they can relate. Use the puppet to lead a discussion that brings application to their own lives.

Keep in mind that children will personally relate to the puppet and its characteristics. Therefore, refrain from allowing a puppet who is acting out bad choices or displaying wrong behavior to be too lovable or appear to be having too much fun, which might encourage imitation. If a puppet pantomimes misbehavior, let the children see the puppet deal with consequences and learn to make better choices. Deal with the wrong behavior and lead a discussion that will help the children relate to similar experiences in their own lives.

Finally, use the puppets to model respect for others. Use respectful language when the puppets address the children, the teachers, the pastor, and other adults.

Clip-n-Teach Puppet Displays

Methods of Displaying and Using Puppets

After putting time and effort into creating the puppets, you will want to give careful attention to methods for storing, displaying, and using them to their greatest advantage. Try some of these suggestions or use your own creativity to come up with your own, innovative system.

Clipping Puppets

One method of displaying puppets is to slide them onto long, spring-action hair clips (similar to clothespins but with long slides that open). Slip the upper slide of the clip into the upper mouth and the bottom slide of the clip into the lower mouth. Attach yarn loops near the spring of the clip for hanging the puppets.

Puppet Trees

Purchase a free-standing, wooden mug holder with several small dowels for hanging mugs. Hang a set of finger puppets on the mug holder, one per dowel.

Hang puppets featuring animals from the nativity on a Christmas tree. Remove the puppets from the tree when using them to tell the story of Christ's birth.

Making Clip-Puppets

Use small squares or circles of Velcro to keep the spring-action clips in place. After sliding the puppet onto the clip, mark places for attaching the Velcro both on the clip and inside the puppet. Remove the clip. Glue the fuzzy sides of the Velcro to the clips and the loopy sides of the Velcro to the inside of the puppet. Slide the clip back in and fasten each piece of Velcro.

Clip-n-Tell Flannel Board Stories

Clip puppets to a flannel board for use when telling a story. Clip the puppets to the board with the heads of the puppets facing away from the audience. Unclip each puppet as needed, turn it around, and use it to tell a particular part of the story. Covering the edge of the flannel board with plastic wrap will help keep the mouths of the puppets clean.

Clip-n-Tell Activities

Clip puppets in accessible places, within easy reach, ready to be used as needed. For example, use a clip-puppet to mark a page in a book so you can easily remove it and use the puppet when that page is turned. Or clip the puppet to an apron, a piece of clothing, or the stage.

Hide a puppet by clipping it on a curtain or another place in the room. Tell the children to hunt for the hidden visitor, then use the puppet as part of your lesson or to tell a story.

Clip puppets to a prop that will be used when teaching a lesson. For example, a puppet can be clipped to a gift as you teach about gifts of God's love, especially the gift of Jesus, our Savior.

Other Group Activities with Puppets

- Plan a mother-daughter tea, making heart puppets for mothers and hand puppets for daughters. Have the moms use their heart puppets to talk about loving their daughters, loving Jesus, and enjoying their daughter's hugs and helping hands. Have the daughters use their hand puppets to talk about giving moms love, hugs, and a helping hand. Provide directions to help participants with the puppet talks. Use paper hearts and hands for decorations too.
- Invite little ones to adopt a senior citizen as a "grandparent" and have the children plan and perform mini-puppet shows for their adopted grandparents.
- Host a puppet camp for children to learn methods of making and using the finger puppets. Teach basic sewing as part of the camp experience.

The Puppet Patterns

Finger Puppet Patterns and Ideas

Refer to the step-by-step directions provided on page 6 as you make each puppet. Follow the suggestions provided to make each puppet unique or let your imagination and creativity go wild.

Cow Puppet

1. Cut a cow from white or light brown felt.
2. Sew or glue the pieces together.
3. Color the horns with a gold or brown fabric marker.
4. Color the spots with a black or brown fabric marker.
5. Color the nostrils with a black fabric marker.
6. Color the inner ear with a pink marker.
7. Glue on movable craft eyes.
8. Cut a red tongue out of felt. Glue the end of the tongue inside the mouth so the tip of the tongue shows when the cow's mouth is closed.

Ideas for Using a Cow Puppet

- Let a cow talk about animals in the stable at Christ's birth (Luke 2).
- Use Psalm 50:10 to teach about greatness, that God's wealth includes the cattle on a thousand hills.
- Design a lesson about generosity, and use the example of giving milk to feed the hungry.
- Teach about talents. Use the analogy of the many ways milk is used to make ice cream, butter, yogurt, cheese, etc.
- Let a cow teach children how a prideful king ate grass as found in Daniel 4:33.
- Let a cow tell the story of the time the Israelites made a golden calf (Exodus 32:1–4).
- Share how Abraham split the land when herdsmen quarreled as found in Genesis 13.
- Use a cow to talk about Pharaoh's dream and Joseph's interpretation of the fat and lean cows (Genesis 41:17–20, 26–27).

Pattern for Cow Puppet

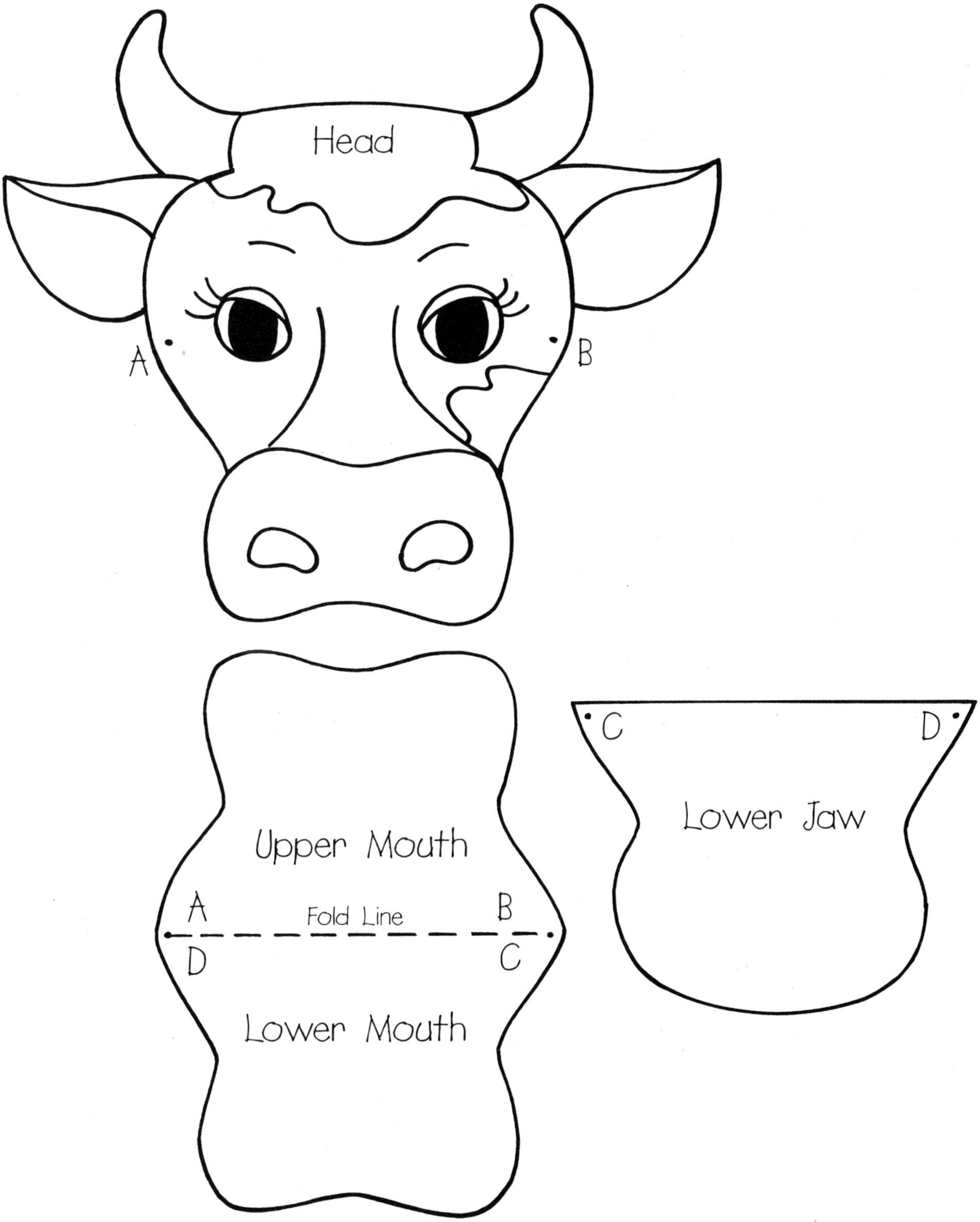

Head

A

B

Upper Mouth

A

Fold Line

B

D

C

Lower Mouth

C

D

Lower Jaw

Pig Puppet

1. Cut a pig from pink felt. Cut the mouth from red felt.
2. Glue or sew the pieces together.
3. Glue the snout piece onto the front of the head. Make nostril marks with a black fabric marker.
4. Glue on movable craft eyes.

Ideas for Using a Pig Puppet

- Teach about problems associated with being sloppy.
- Relate the concept of wallowing in mud to being stuck in sin and bad habits.
- Tell the story of the prodigal son from the pig's perspective. Relate what the son might have said to the pigs (Luke 15:11–32).
- Share how Jesus cast out demons and sent them into 70 pigs. The demons drove the pigs crazy and into the sea (Mark 5:11–13).
- Talk about the fact that pigs do not sweat. In hot weather a pig needs water or mud to cool off or it could die. Let a pig puppet talk about being too hot and tell the story of the rich man and Lazarus (Luke 16:19–31).
- Use a pig puppet to talk about junk food. A pig only eats food that is good for it. Let a pig talk about healthy food and discourage eating junk food.

Pattern for Pig Puppet

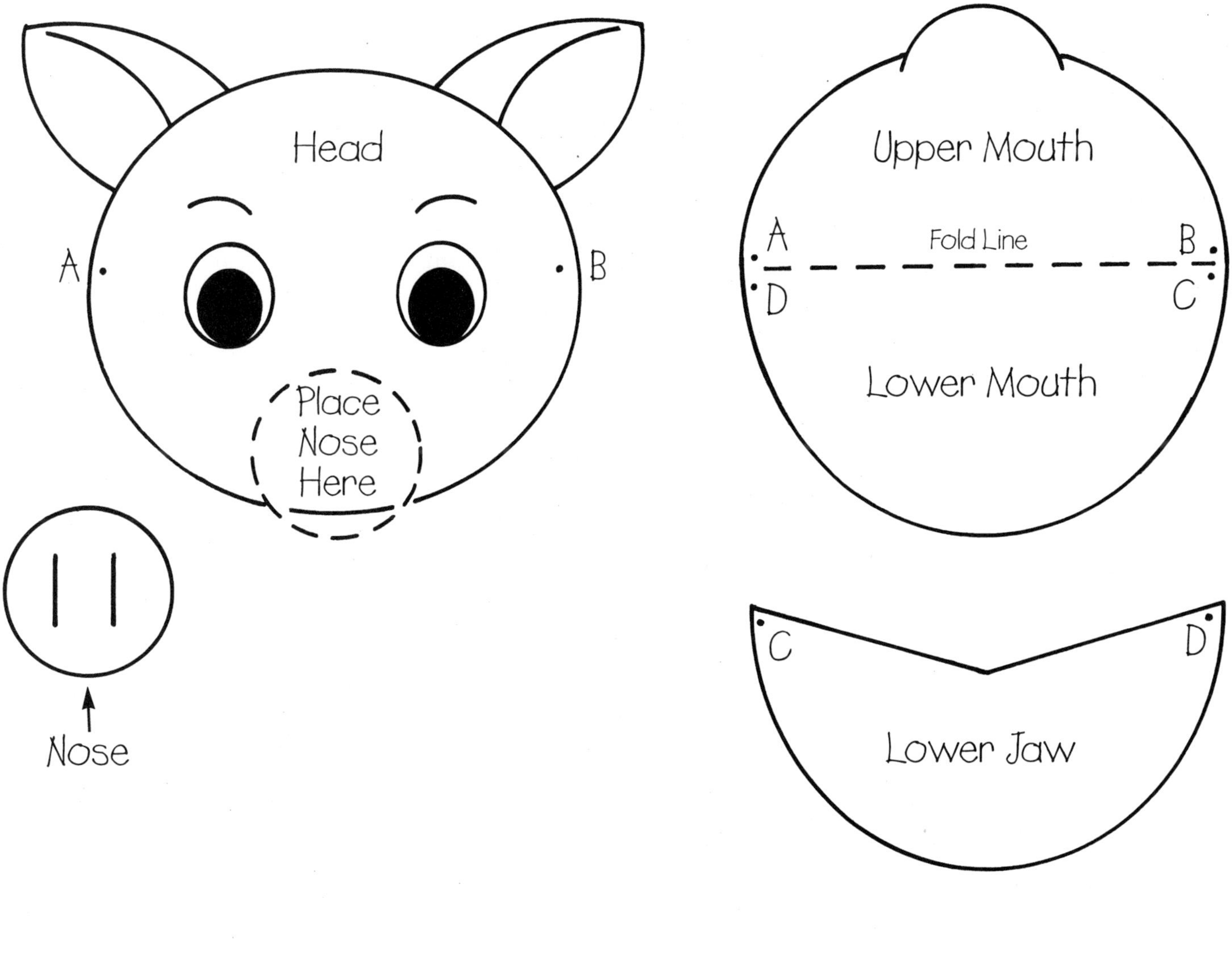

Head

A

B

Place Nose Here

Nose

Upper Mouth

A

Fold Line

B

D

C

Lower Mouth

C

D

Lower Jaw

Oyster Puppet

1. Cut an oyster from beige or light gray felt.
2. Assemble the puppet according to the step-by-step directions.
3. Glue or sew a white pearl bead inside the oyster's mouth. Glue on eyes.

Ideas for Using an Oyster Puppet

- Teach about heaven and the pearl of great value as found in Matthew 13:45–46.
- Share how an oyster spins a pearl, turning an irritation into something beautiful. Relate this to God using all things for our good as found in Romans 8:28.
- Let an oyster talk about the protection of shells and the value of God's protection.
- Let an oyster share the story of Jesus calming the storm at sea (Matthew 8:26).
- An oyster's shape is irregular and the shell is bumpy, yet inside the oyster spins a beautiful pearl and the lining of the shell is smooth. Talk about how God cares more about inner beauty as referenced in Psalm 139:15–16, 23.

Fascinating Oyster Facts

- Oysters work slowly. It may take an oyster three years to produce one pearl!
- Oysters live in oyster beds. This is an area in the ocean covered with old empty oyster shells, called an oyster reef, where oysters live together in groups, or colonies.
- Millions of oysters are born each year but few survive for very long because the oyster becomes food for many sea creatures and for people.

Pattern for Oyster Puppet

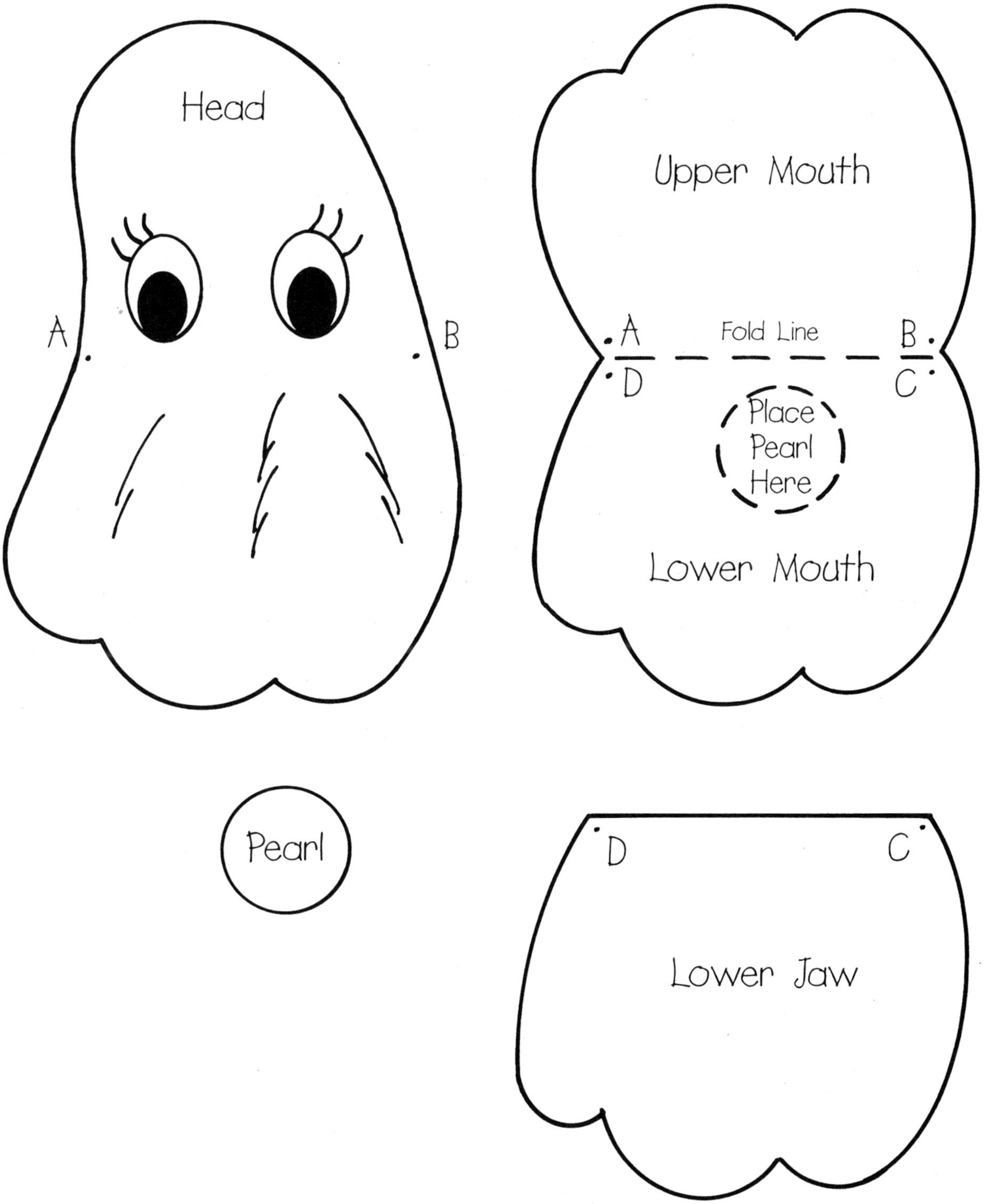

Head

A

B

Upper Mouth

A Fold Line B

D C

Place Pearl Here

Lower Mouth

Pearl

D C

Lower Jaw

Camel Puppet

1. Cut a camel from tan or camel-colored felt.
2. Use brown fur or brown yarn to sew a beard between the lower jaw and the mouth.
3. Assemble the puppet according to the step-by-step directions.
4. Glue or sew metallic gold trim on forehead. This gives the impression of a sheik's headpiece.
5. Add eyes.

Ideas for Using a Camel Puppet

- Let a camel teach about traveling in caravans with Bible characters such as Abraham or the Wise Men.
- Teach about the value of water and how important it is to be prepared for difficult times.
- Share how camels have special hooves for walking on sand. Relate the camel's feet to God giving us what we need according to His purposes.
- Use a camel puppet to explain the illustration Jesus uses comparing how it is easier for a camel to go through the eye of a needle than it is for the rich man to enter heaven (Matthew 19:24).
- Share the importance of bringing gifts to others. Discuss the gifts the Wise Men, who probably rode camels, brought to Jesus (Matthew 2:1–12). Discuss the types of gifts we bring to Jesus in gratitude for His saving love for us.
- Let a camel talk about the comparison of following the star and following Christ as referenced in Matthew 2:9 and Matthew 4:19.
- Let a camel share the story of the servant who found a bride for Isaac as she watered camels (Genesis 24:11–27).

Pattern for Camel Puppet

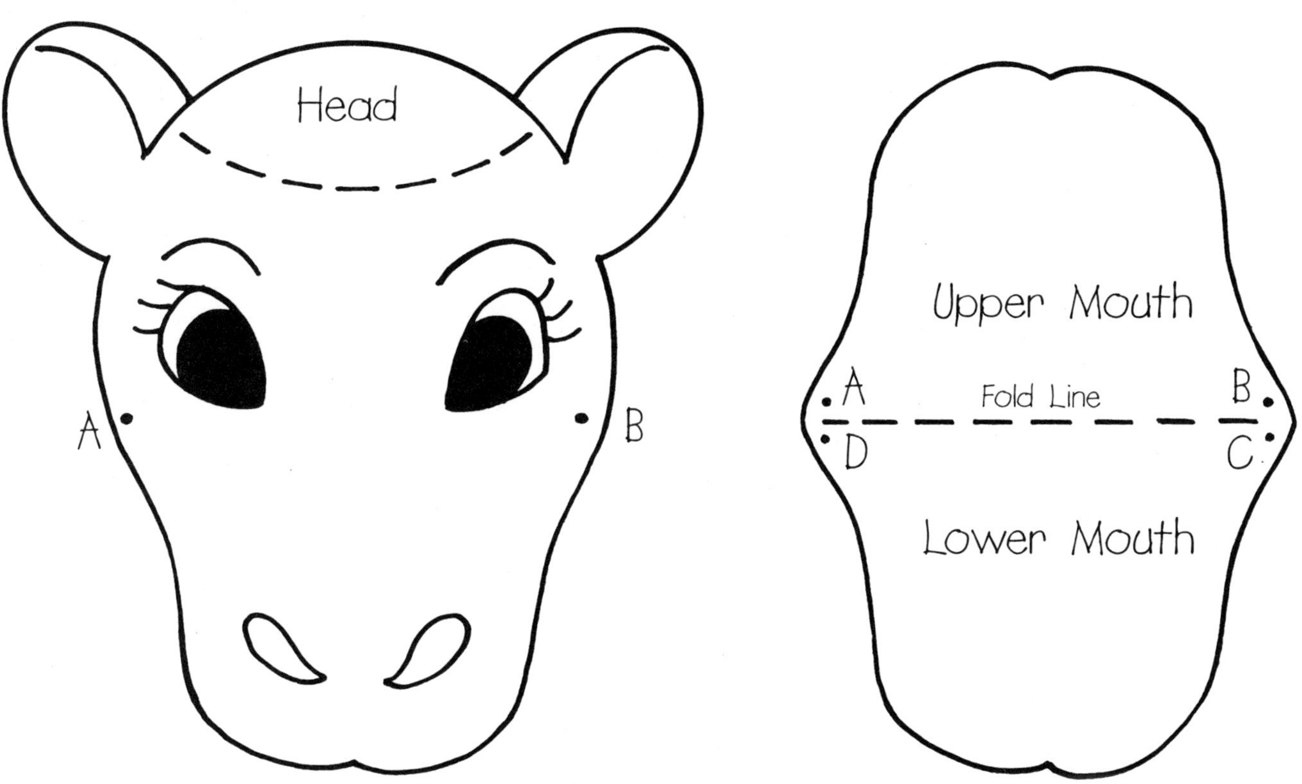

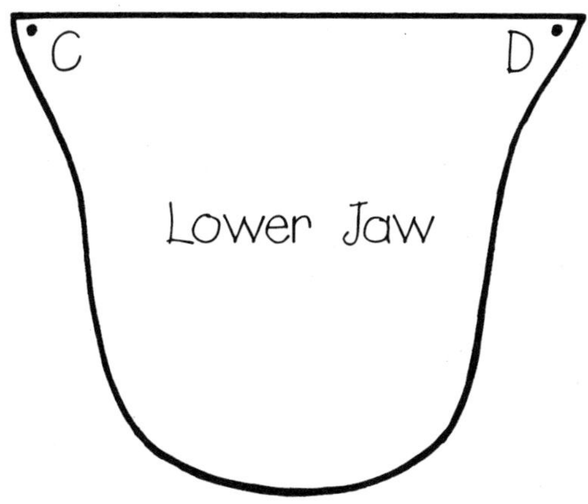

Lamb Puppet

1. Cut a lamb from white or black felt.
2. Assemble the puppet according to the step-by-step directions.
3. Add a tiny pink pompom nose.
4. Glue on eyes.
5. Add curly yarn to the forehead for hair. Sew a pink felt tongue inside the mouth.

Ideas for Using a Lamb Puppet

- Use a lamb puppet to teach about Jesus, the Good Shepherd, as found in John 10:11–18.
- Let a lamb lead a discussion of how the Lord's care for His children is like a shepherd's care for his sheep as referenced in Isaiah 40:11, Jeremiah 31:10, and Ezekiel 34:11–16.
- Share how a lamb's wool provides warmth and clothing. Thank God for creating lambs. Talk about how this is one example of a way God provides for our needs as referenced in Matthew 6:31–34. What other ways does He provide for us?
- Let a lamb tell the parable of the lost sheep (Luke 15:1–7).
- Talk about the significance of Christ being called the Lamb of God (1 Peter 1:17–21).
- Let a lamb talk about Psalm 23 and teach about how one day a lamb will eat with a wolf in the new heaven and the new earth as referenced in Isaiah 65:25.
- Let a lamb talk about King David as a shepherd (1 Samuel 16:11).

Pattern for Lamb Puppet

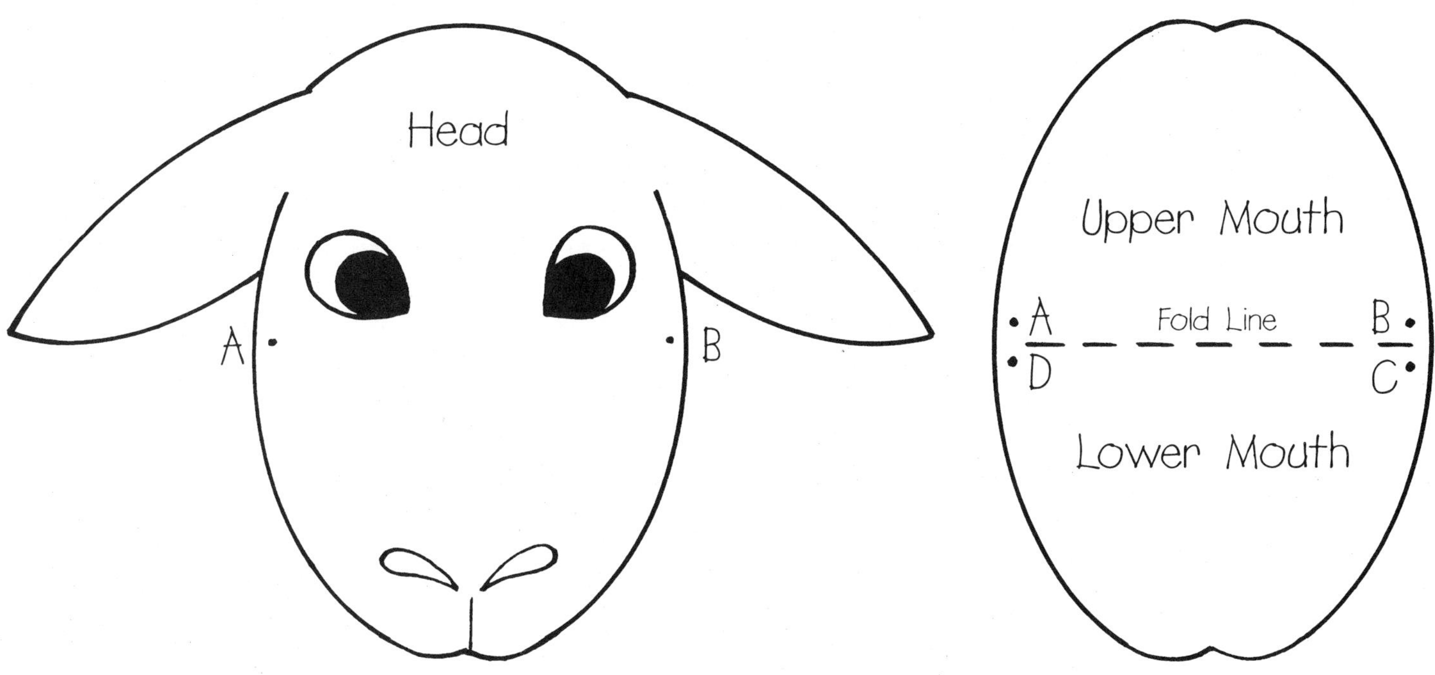

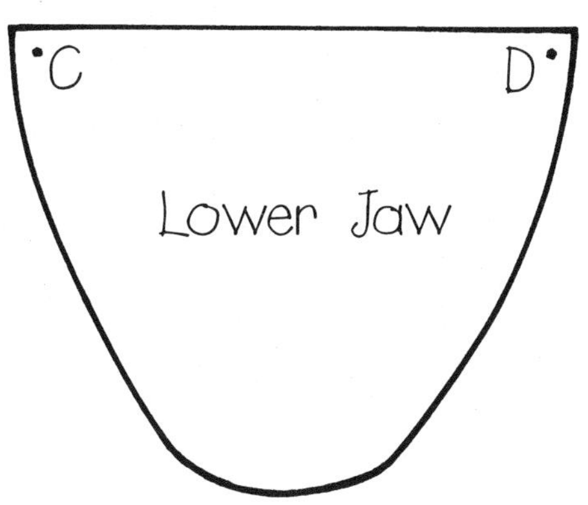

Bear Puppet

1. Cut a bear from brown fuzzy felt.
2. Assemble the puppet according to the step-by-step directions.
3. Add a black pompom for a nose.
4. Add eyes.
5. (Optional) Use white and black felt to make a panda bear or all white for a polar bear.

Ideas for Using a Bear Puppet

- Let the bear puppet tell how David fought a bear as told in 1 Samuel 17:34–37.
- Talk about a bear's desire for honey to help the children understand the reference to the sweetness of God's words as mentioned in Psalm 19:10.
- Let a tree-climbing bear tell the tale of Zacchaeus, Luke 19:1–10.
- Teach about the future peace that will be ours through Christ, when harmony will be restored and a bear will lie with a cow (Isaiah 11:7).
- Panda bears eat only bamboo. Have a panda bear puppet talk about being picky about what our eyes see and our ears hear as we follow Jesus and live according to God's Word.
- Contrast the state of sin (people growling like bears in Isaiah 59:11) with living our lives as children of God (Philippians 2:14).
- Bears fish well. Discuss how the Holy Spirit works in us to help us become fishers of men (Matthew 4:19).

Pattern for Bear Puppet

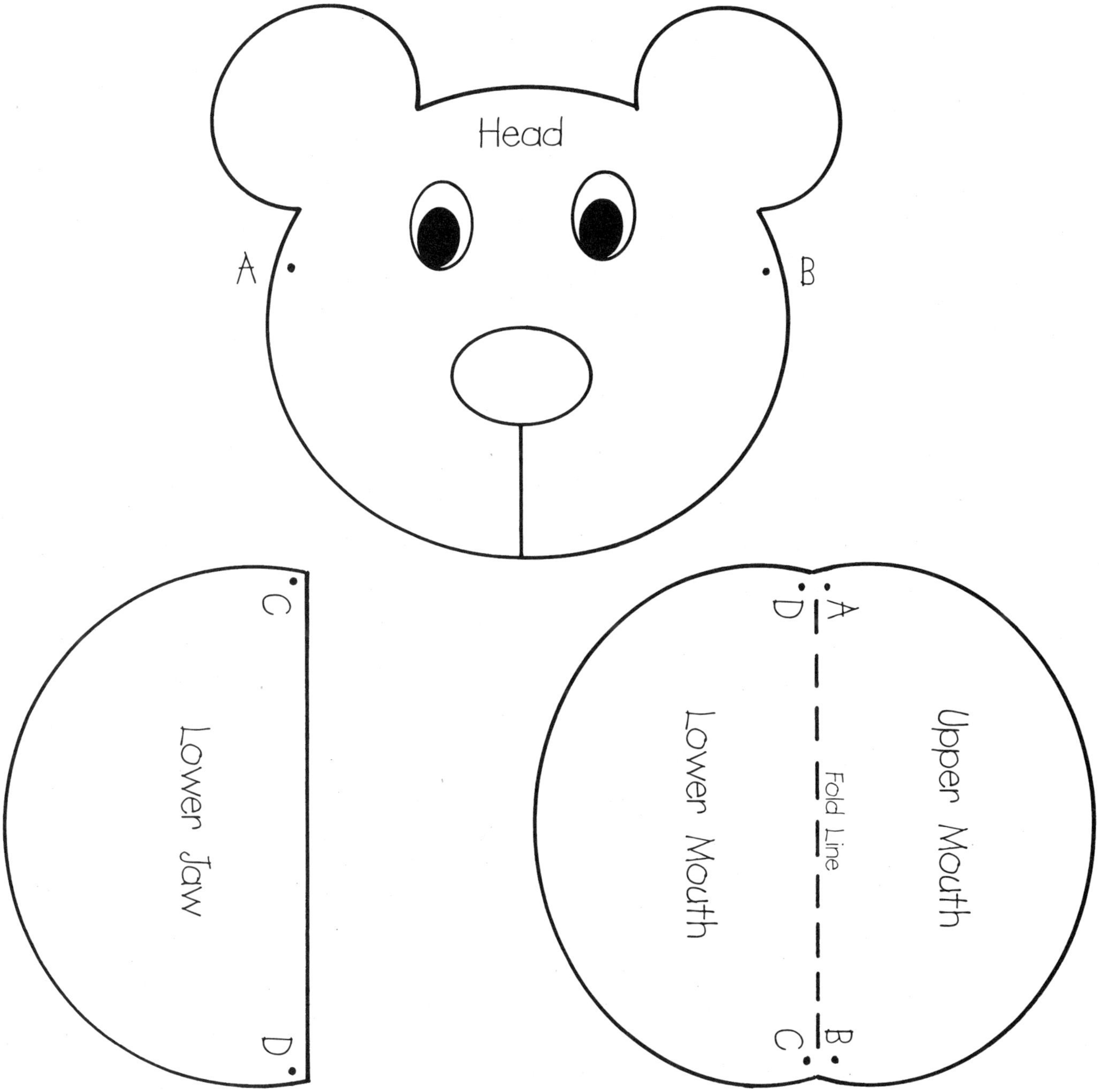

Frog Puppet

1. Cut a frog from green felt.
2. Cut a tongue from orange felt.
3. Cut two yellow background circles from craft foam to use for the eyes.
4. Assemble the puppet according to the step-by-step directions.
5. Glue a tongue inside the mouth.
6. Glue the two circles cut from foam onto the head. Glue eyes onto the foam circles.

Ideas for Using a Frog Puppet

- Teach about the plague of frogs as told in Exodus 8:2–11.
- Let a frog teach about enjoying nature and relate the story of creation as found in Genesis 1.
- Share how a frog does not let little things be bothersome— the frog eats what bugs him. A frog can help explain being content (Philippians 4:12–13).
- Talk about water heating up as a frog sits in it. Compare that to the destructive nature of complacency (Proverbs 1:32).
- Use a frog to lead children in songs of praise and jumping for joy. Explain the benefits of a joyful heart (Proverbs 17:22).
- Let a frog tell what it means to be green with envy. Contrast that to love that grows out of a will to love in obedience to God's command (1 Corinthians 13:4).
- A frog with good eyesight can teach about seeing well. Compare that to eyes of faith that see and believe (Matthew 13:16).

Pattern for Frog Puppet

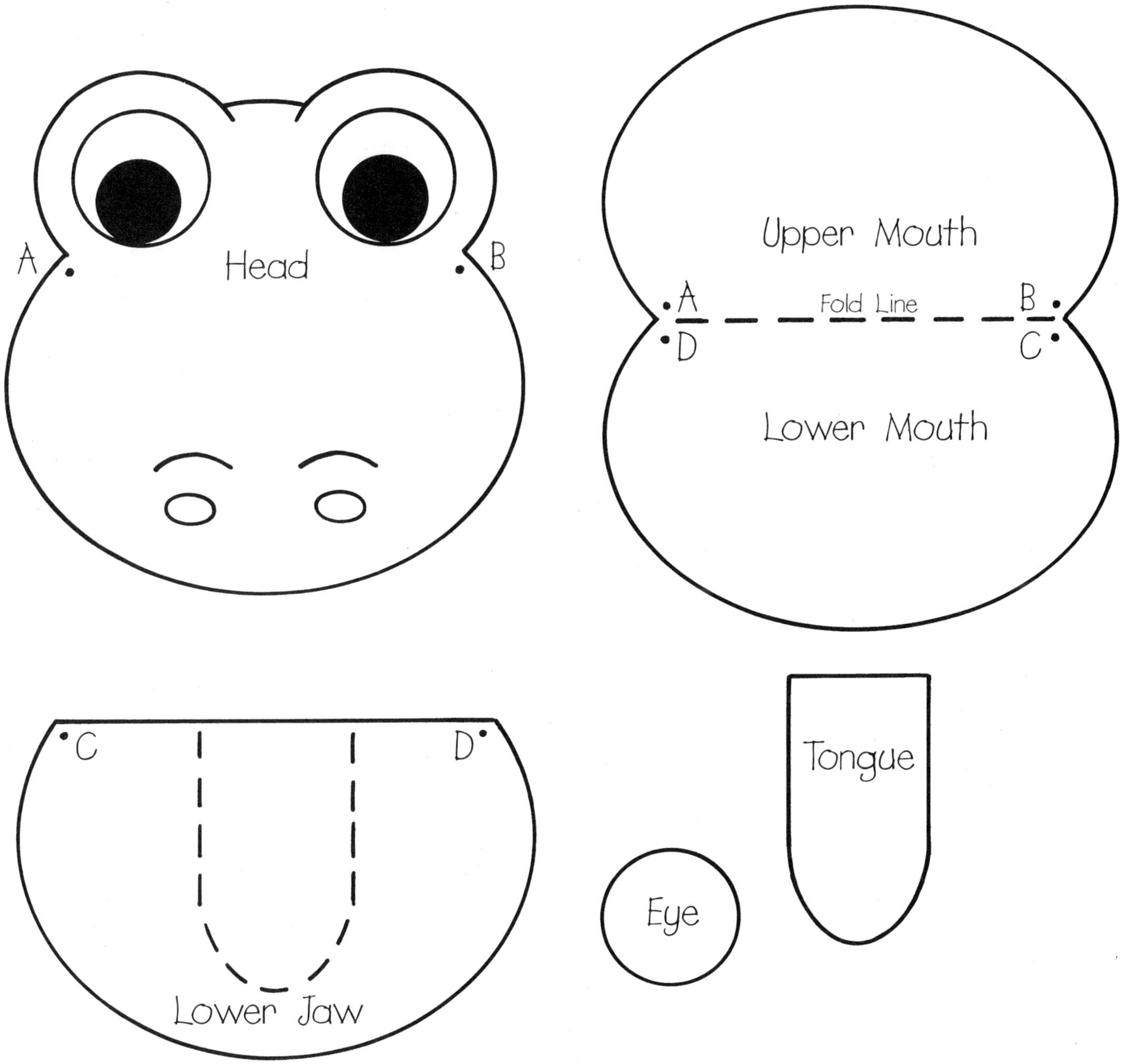

A Head B

Upper Mouth

A Fold Line B

D C

Lower Mouth

C D

Lower Jaw

Tongue

Eye

Donkey Puppet

1. Cut a donkey from gray or brown felt.
2. Cut nostrils and hair from black felt. Fringe the felt for hair.
3. Cut teeth from white craft foam.
4. Assemble the puppet according to the step-by-step directions.
5. Add hair and nostrils.
6. Glue the teeth along the front of the upper jaw.

Ideas for Using a Donkey Puppet

- Let a donkey talk about the ride of Jesus into Jerusalem on Palm Sunday (Matthew 21:1–11).
- Share how a donkey spoke to Balaam (Numbers 22:28–32).
- Relate the stubbornness of a donkey to the stubbornness and hard hearts of people. Discuss how God changes hearts (Ezekiel 11:19–20).
- Let a donkey teach about Deborah's praise and a white donkey (Judges 5:10).
- Use a donkey to tell how Saul met the prophet Samuel and became king of the Israelites while looking for lost donkeys (1 Samuel 9: 1–17).
- Use a donkey to tell how Abigail brought gifts to King David on donkeys and how she helped feed David and his men (1 Samuel 25:18–35).

Pattern for Donkey Puppet

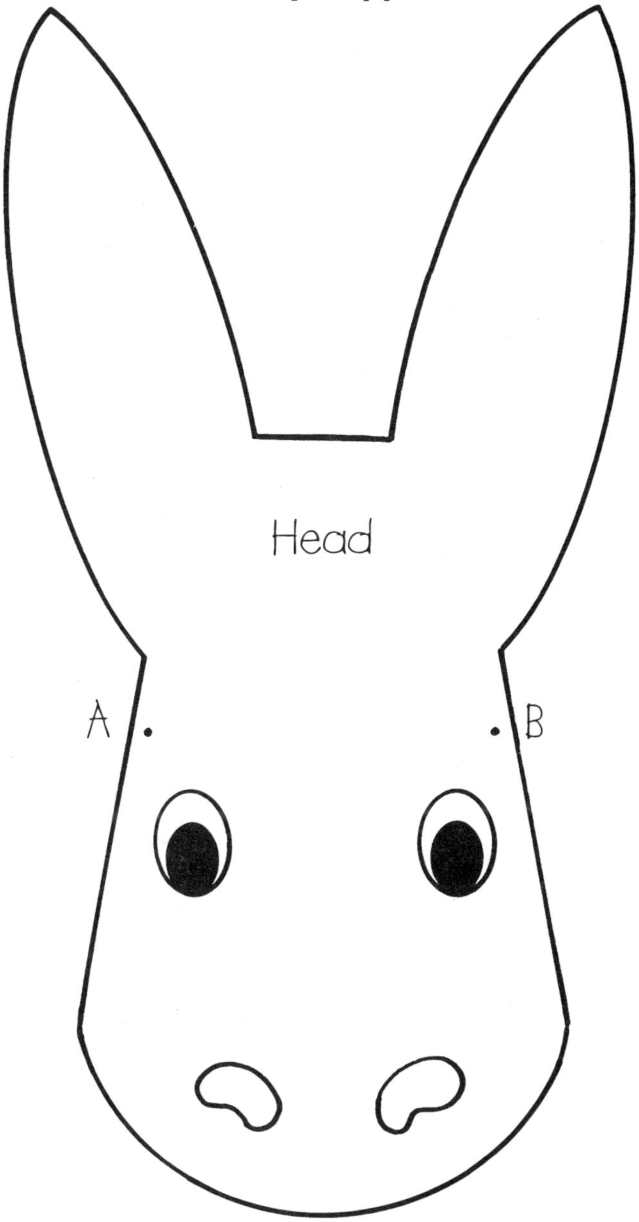

Head

A

B

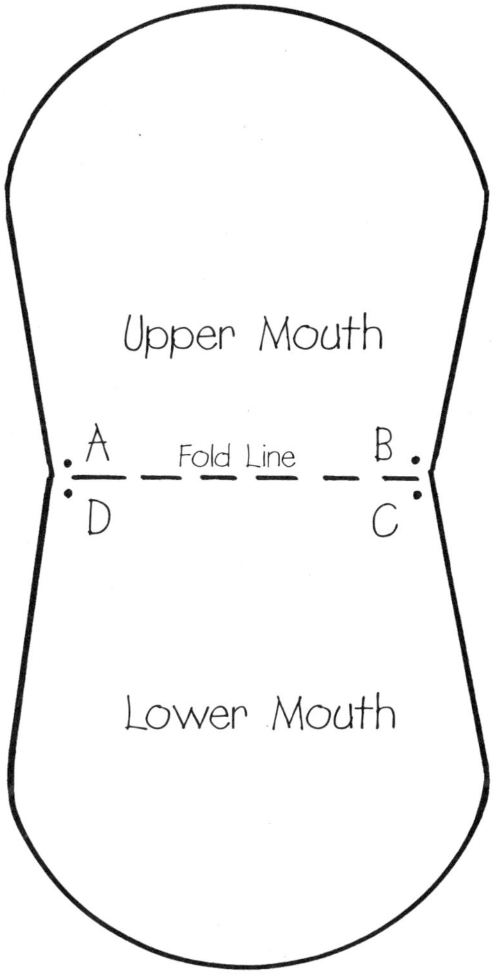

Upper Mouth

A

Fold Line

B

D

C

Lower Mouth

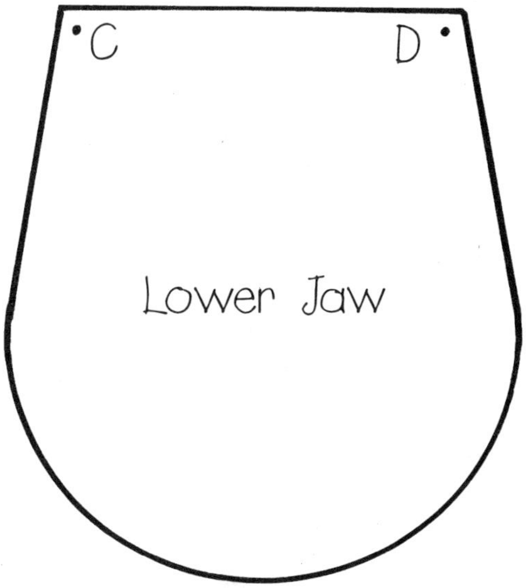

C

D

Lower Jaw

Mouse Puppet

1. Cut a mouse from white or gray felt.
2. Assemble the puppet according to the step-by-step directions.
3. Add whiskers using yarn or stamens from artificial flowers.
4. Add eyes.
5. (Optional) Add pink felt to the inside of the ears.

Ideas for Using a Mouse Puppet

- Use a mouse to talk about quiet, respectful behavior as referenced in 1 Timothy 2:2.
- Tell the children that mice eat paper. Read about Ezekiel, who actually ate a scroll (Ezekiel 3:1–3). Discuss that God's children digest Scripture by hearing God's Word and learning it.
- Let a mouse be nervous around a mousetrap. Discuss avoiding temptations and praying to God for deliverance from evil (Matthew 6:13).
- Discuss how people are often afraid of a tiny mouse. Use the mouse to teach about trusting in God for protection (Psalm 91).
- Discuss how a mouse learns to find its way through a maze. Tell the children that Jesus is the only way to heaven—the Way, the Truth, and the Life, as found in John 14:6.
- Share the fact that a mouse is small enough to hold in the palm of our hand. The Bible tells us that God holds us and guides us (Psalm 139:10) and sends angels to carry us (Psalm 91:11–12).
- Let a church mouse lead singing (Psalm 148).
- Mice eat grain. Let a mouse ask questions about the need for Jesus, the Bread of Life (John 6:35, 51).

Pattern for Mouse Puppet

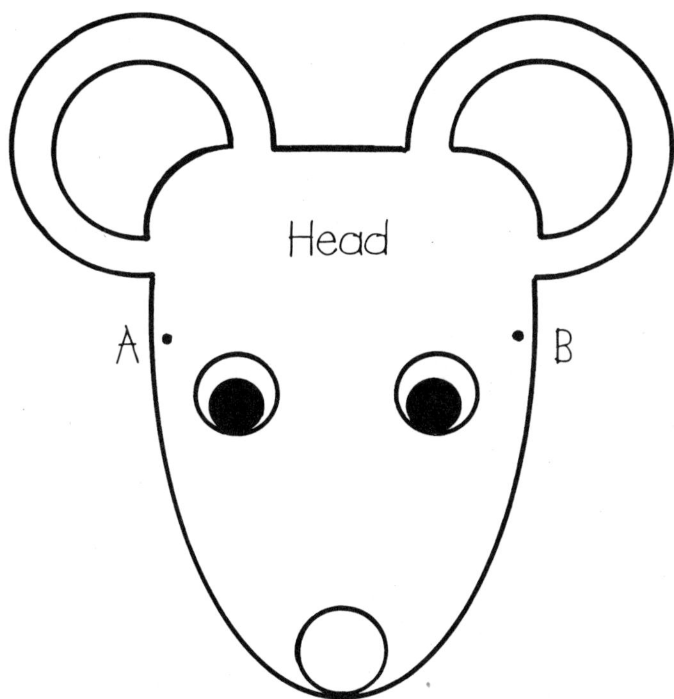

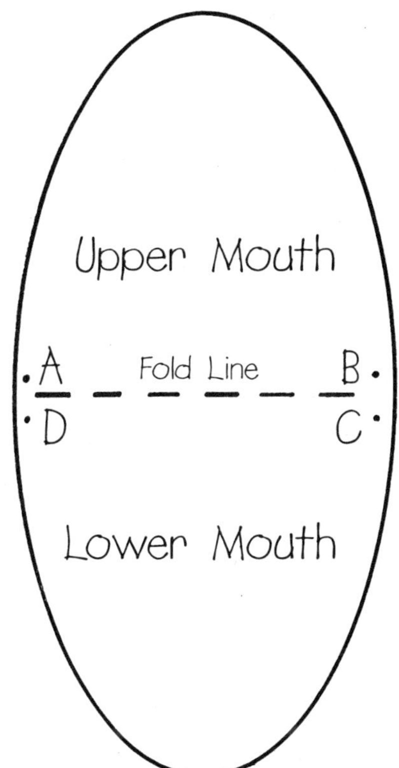

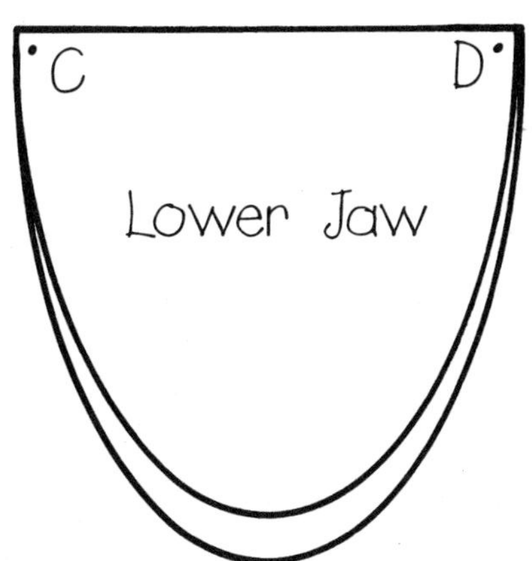

Elephant Puppet

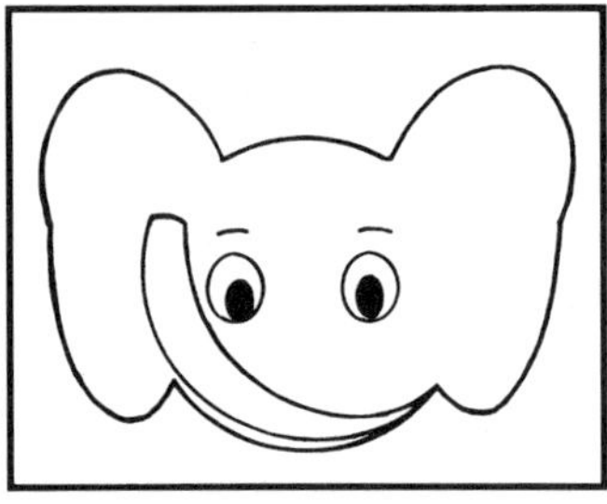

1. Cut an elephant head and lower jaw from gray felt.
2. Cut the mouth from pink felt.
3. Assemble the puppet according to the step-by-step directions.
4. Cut a 2-inch piece of chenille stem. Starting at the tip of the trunk, glue the chenille stem to the underside of the trunk, centering it on the piece of felt. Bend the trunk up as desired.
5. Glue on eyes.
6. (Optional) Cut tusks from felt or craft foam and glue them on the elephant.

Ideas for Using an Elephant Puppet

- Let an elephant talk about wise King Solomon, who had a throne of ivory, as found in 1 Kings 10:18, 23.
- An elephant can be kept captive by a little peg. This will happen if a peg restrains the elephant as a baby. After that, the elephant never tests the peg again. People often believe they are trapped by sin or a habit and do not use God's help to break free. Read John 8:31–32 to discover how to be free.
- An elephant raises its trunk and gives a trumpet blast in joy. Let an elephant puppet lead others in a musical praise party (Psalm 150).
- Let an elephant teach about the importance of remembering Scripture (Psalm 119:11).
- An elephant can pull a lot of weight and do lots of work. Discuss working hard for the Lord (1 Timothy 6:18). Talk about Paul's work for the Lord (Acts 20:34–35).

Pattern for Elephant Puppet

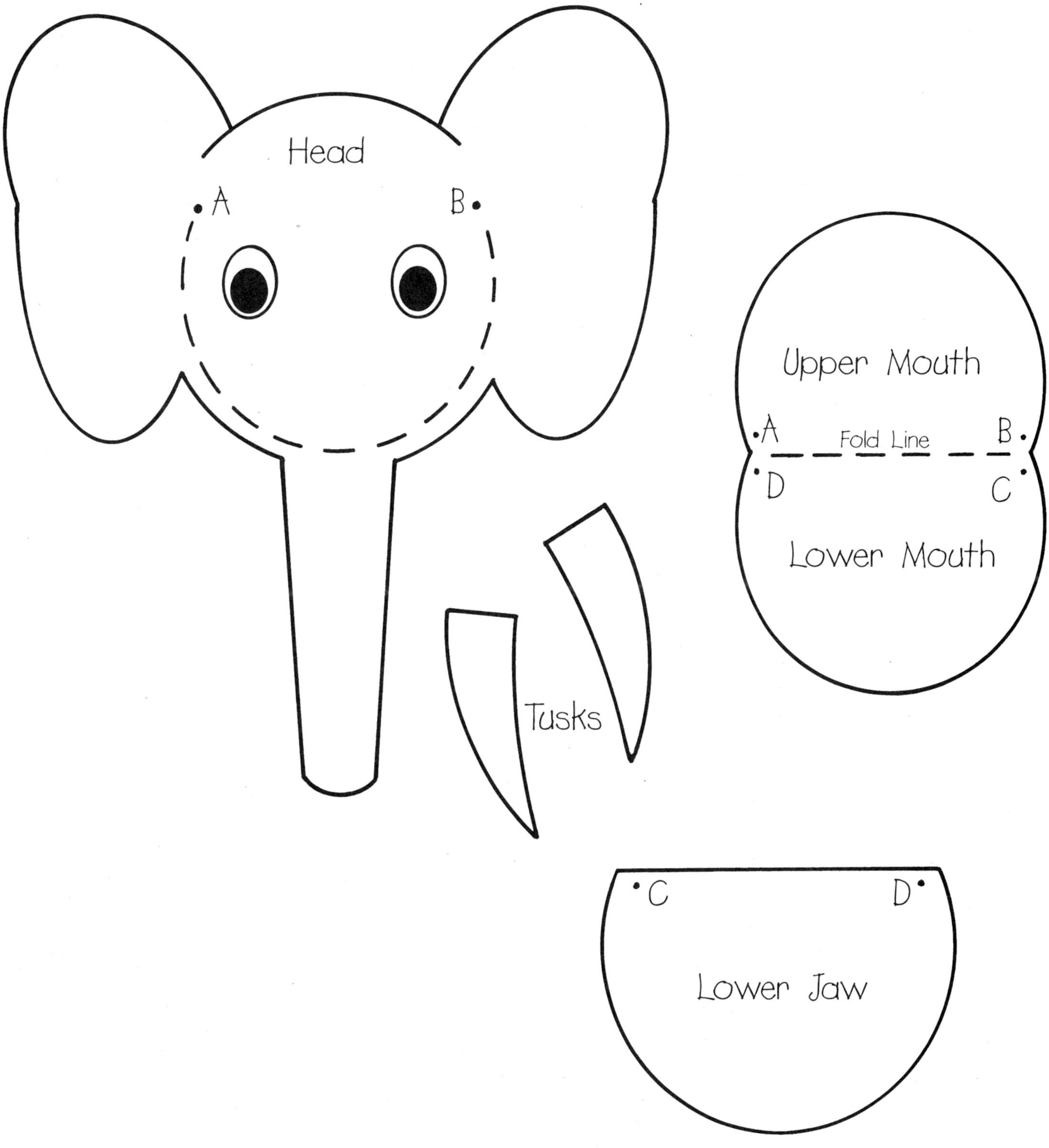

Head

A B

Upper Mouth

A Fold Line B

D C

Lower Mouth

Tusks

C D

Lower Jaw

Jellyfish Puppet

1. Cut a jellyfish from white or light blue felt.
2. Sew and gather the upper head of the jellyfish. Stuff it with polyfill.
3. Sew the upper head to the lower headpiece.
4. Cut several 6-inch lengths of yarn for tentacles.
5. Sew the tentacles between the lower jaw and mouth.
6. Assemble the puppet according to the step-by-step directions.
7. Add small eyes to the front of the head.

Ideas for Using a Jellyfish Puppet

- Use a jellyfish to teach about the dangers of giving in to peer pressure and going with the flow (James 1:5–6).
- Let a jellyfish talk about the harm of stinging words (Proverbs 15:1).
- Share how God made all sorts of fascinating sea creatures (Psalm 104:24–25).
- Let a jellyfish describe its bell. Praise God using bells (Exodus 28:33–35).

Fascinating Jellyfish Facts

- The bell-shaped body of a jellyfish is called a bell.
- Some jellyfish can actually swim, but many just drift with the current.
- Some jellyfish contract the bell's margin to expel water and move by a type of jet propulsion.
- Jellyfish can be from .12 inches to 6½ feet in diameter!

Pattern for Jellyfish Puppet

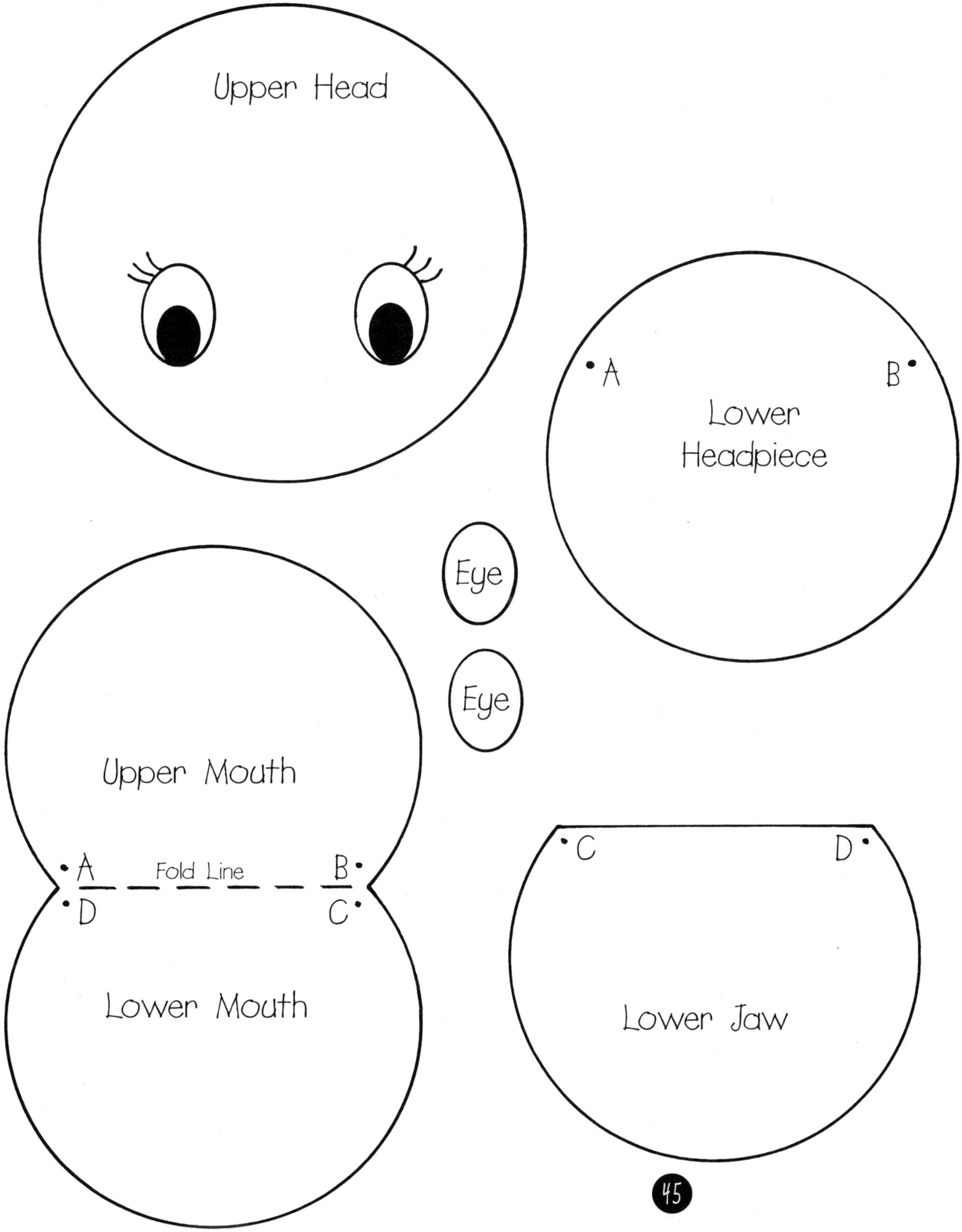

Upper Head

Lower Headpiece

A B

Eye

Eye

Upper Mouth

A Fold Line B

D C

Lower Mouth

Lower Jaw

C D

Canadian Goose Puppet

1. Cut a goose from black felt.
2. Cut the goose trim from white felt or paint the parts of trim white.
3. Glue or sew the white trim as indicated in pattern.
4. Assemble the puppet according to the step-by-step directions.
5. Add small eyes.

Ideas for Using a Canadian Goose Puppet

- Canadian geese fly in a "V" formation, giving them strength and adding 71 percent greater flying range. Let a goose tell children about the symbol "V" for victory and working together in unity (Ephesians 4:16).
- Let a Canadian goose talk about the instinct that leads them and compare that to sharing God's Word as referenced in Jeremiah 8:7.
- A goose mates only one time, for life, unless his mate dies. Jesus spoke of the faithfulness of marriage in Matthew 19:6.
- Two geese will help a goose that is hurt. Read about helping others in Galatians 6:2.
- When the lead goose gets tired, another goose will take the lead. These geese are serving one another, helping the whole group. Compare this to Galatians 5:13–14.
- Geese honk to encourage one another. Talk about encouraging others, as directed in 1 Thessalonians 5:11.

Pattern for Canadian Goose Puppet

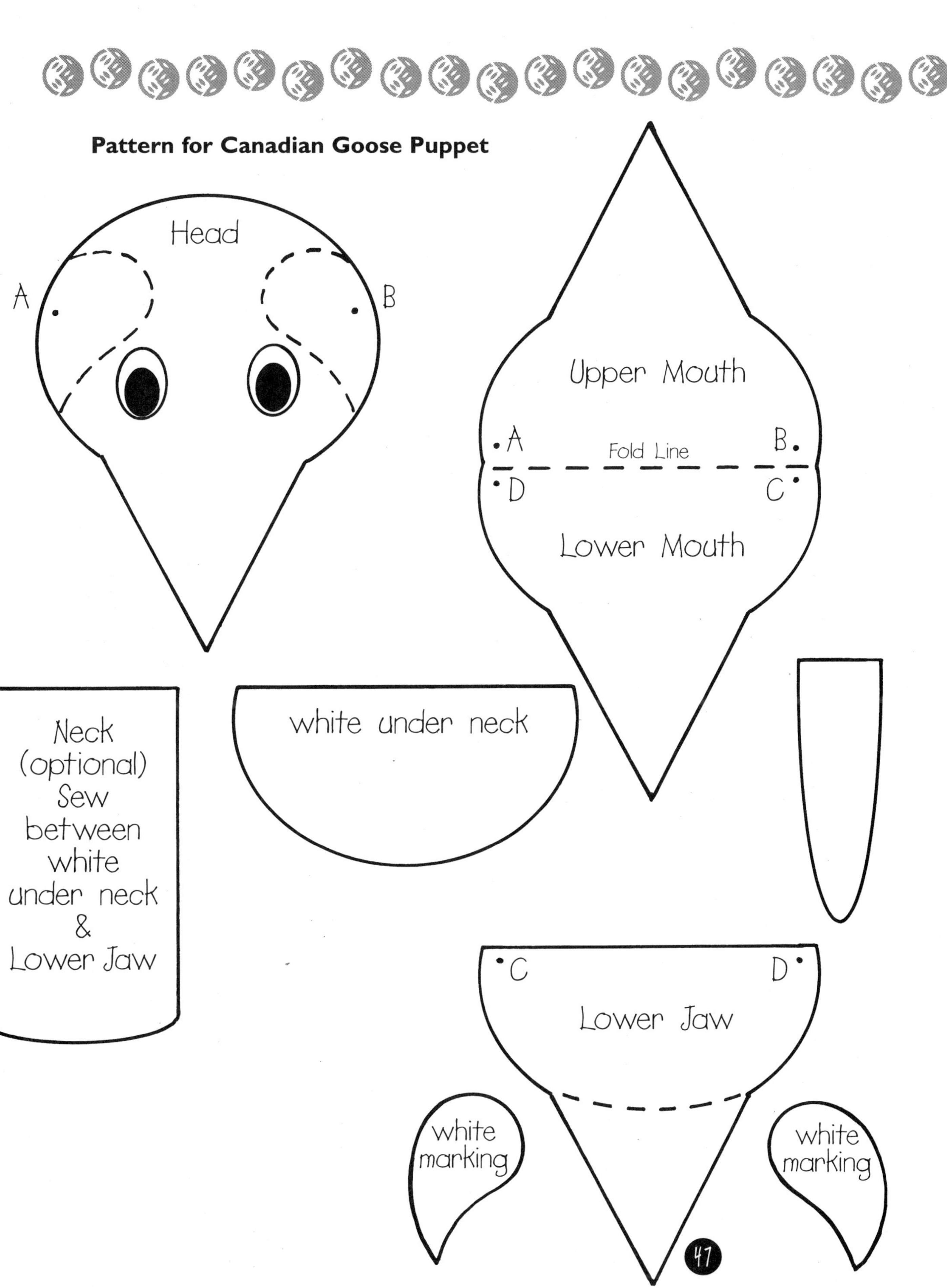

Lion Puppet

1. Cut a lion from yellow or gold felt.
2. Buy a piece of yellow fringe and cut it long enough to fit around the lion's head.
3. Sew the fringe around the head.
4. Assemble the puppet according to the step-by-step directions.
5. Add a small, brown pompom nose and yarn whiskers.
6. Add a tongue cut from orange or pink felt.
7. Add eyes.

Ideas for Using a Lion Puppet

- Tell how lions did not harm a believer because of God's protection (Daniel 6:16–24).
- Compare the strength of the friendship between David and Jonathan to a lion's strength (2 Samuel 1:23).
- Let a lion explain why the tribe of Judah is called a lion (Genesis 49:9–10).
- Teach how David learned to trust God when he faced a lion (1 Samuel 17:34).
- Share how a lion is brave and mighty (Proverbs 30:29–30).
- Try to solve Samson's riddle about honey and a lion (Judges 14:6–14).
- Relate how the devil is like a prowling lion (1 Peter 5:8).
- Discuss Proverbs 28:1, which references the righteous being bold as a lion.
- Let a lion talk about the signal of God's roar to His people in Hosea 11:10.

Pattern for Lion Puppet

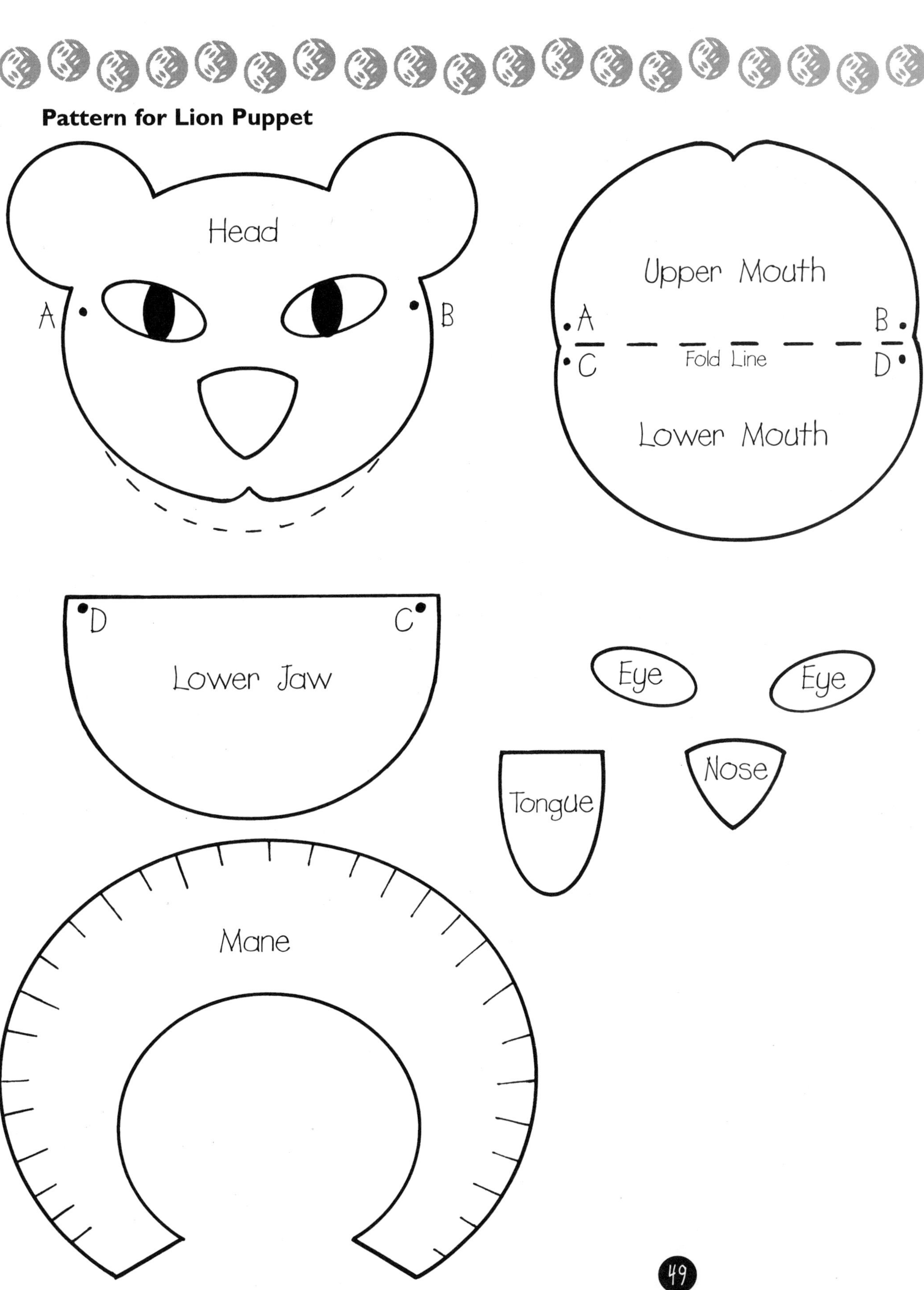

Dog Puppet

1. Cut a dog from brown, white, or black felt. Using fuzzy felt will give the dog a long-haired look.
2. Assemble the puppet according to the step-by-step directions.
3. Add a small, black pompom nose.
4. Add eyes.

Ideas for Using a Dog Puppet

- Let a dog teach about friendship and how someone can stick to you closer than a brother (Proverbs 18:24).
- Use a dog to tell the story of the Canaanite woman who asked Jesus to heal her daughter. She spoke about feeding bread crumbs to dogs (Matthew 15:26–27).
- Discuss love and care for pets (Proverbs 12:10).
- Talk about the ways a dog learns to obey a master. Let a dog give pointers on obeying parents (Ephesians 6:1).
- Discuss seeing-eye dogs. Talk about the Holy Spirit who guides us (John 16:13).
- Talk about how a dog follows his master (heeling). Discuss the ways the disciples followed Jesus (Matthew 4:20).

Pattern for the Dog Puppet

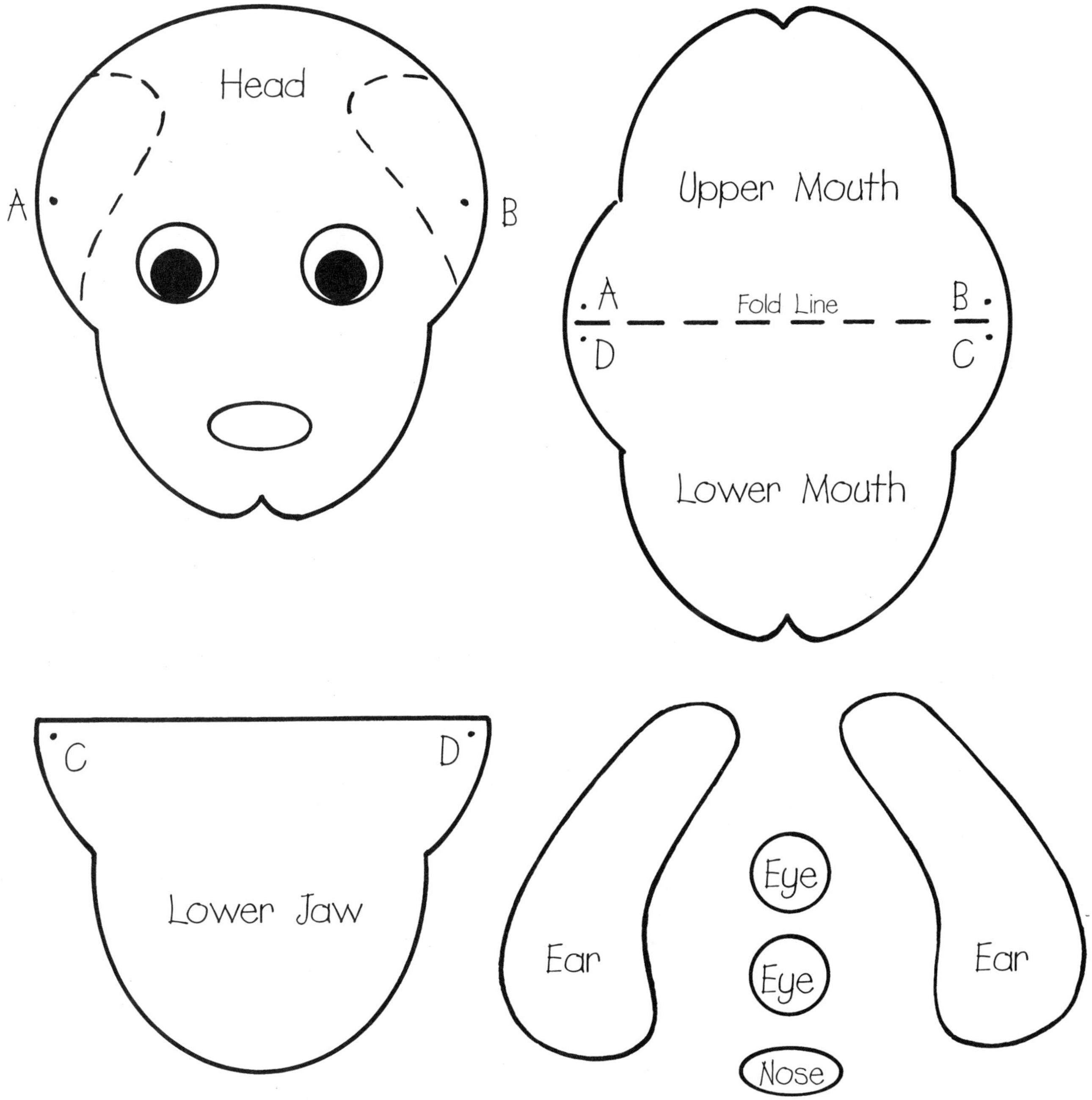

Head

A B

Upper Mouth

A Fold Line B

D C

Lower Mouth

C D

Lower Jaw

Ear

Eye

Eye

Nose

Ear

Bible Puppet

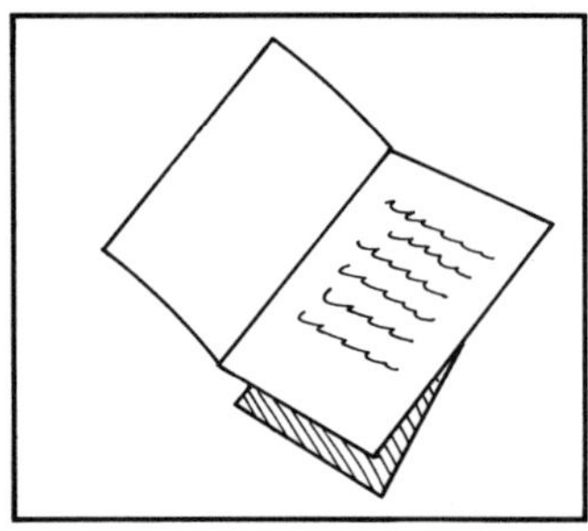

1. Cut the cover and back of the Bible from black or red felt.
2. Cut a mouth from white felt.
3. (Optional) To make a secret page to use for a Bible verse or message, cut a second cover from white felt. Sew this to the upper mouth as the puppet's head. Attach the red or black cover to the white page, sewing only along the binding side of the book. Add Velcro to the upper right corner to keep the book closed. Pin a verse reference on the inside and open the Bible to show the verse.
4. To make a Bible without a secret page, sew or glue the puppet together using the general, step-by-step directions.
5. Write BIBLE across the front. Use a fabric marker or paint to make a cross at the lower edge for a nose.
6. Glue movable craft eyes over the lower circles of the Bs, forming eyes.

Ideas for Using a Bible Puppet

- Let the puppet share Bible verses and talk about the importance of treasuring God's Word (Psalm 119:11).
- Explain how to find a verse in the Bible and ways to study Scripture (Acts 17:11).
- Introduce Bible lessons or biblical people (2 Timothy 3:16).
- Let a Bible puppet share thoughts about the sharpness of the Word (Hebrews 4:12).

Pattern for Bible Puppet

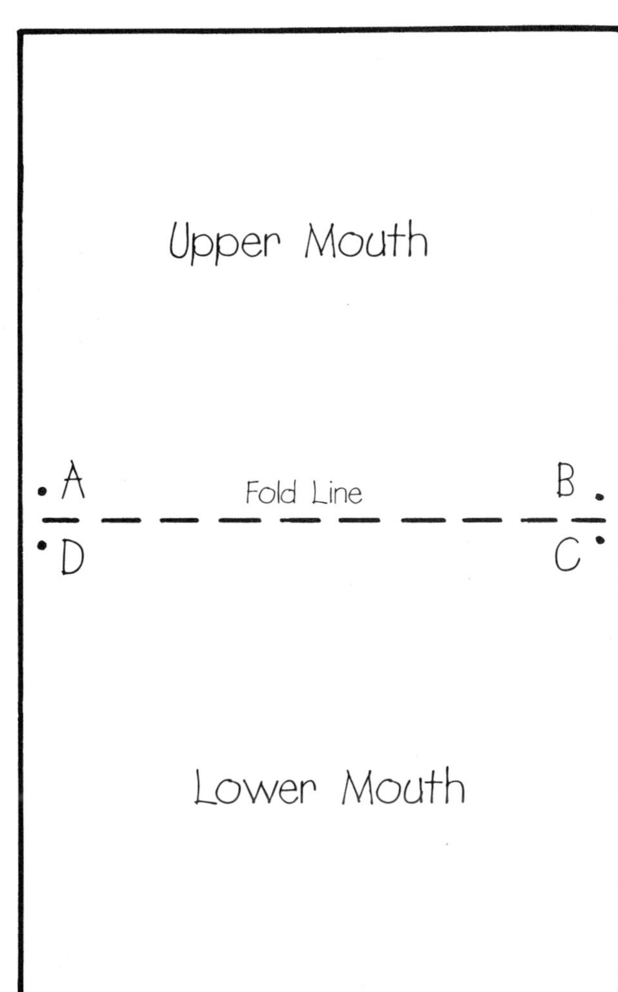

Foot Puppet (Make Two)      

1. Cut two feet from felt. Cut one set for the left foot and invert the patterns for the right foot. Cut fabric along the dotted line to make the head and lower jaw. *Note: Cut the toes of the head and lower jaw after sewing.*
2. Sew or glue the pieces together.
3. Paint the toenails with a fabric marker or fabric paint.
4. Glue movable craft eyes on each foot.

Ideas for Using Foot Puppets

- Teach about the places Bible people traveled with their feet (Jonah 1:3).
- Let a puppet discuss the harmful behavior of feet, such as kicking, arriving late, etc.
- Use a puppet to tell how Jesus healed those who were crippled (Mark 2:3–12).
- Teach about running a race. Compare that to 1 Corinthians 9:24–25.
- Talk about the time Moses stood on holy ground (Exodus 3:5).
- Let a foot puppet demonstrate how to leap or dance with joy (Exodus 15:20–21).
- Let a puppet talk about the feet Jesus washed in John 13:5 or the time Mary Magdalene washed the feet of Jesus with her tears in Luke 7:38.
- Talk about ways feet can bring the Good News to others (Romans 10:15).
- Have children tell what they'll do this week as amazing feats of feet.

Pattern for the Foot Puppet

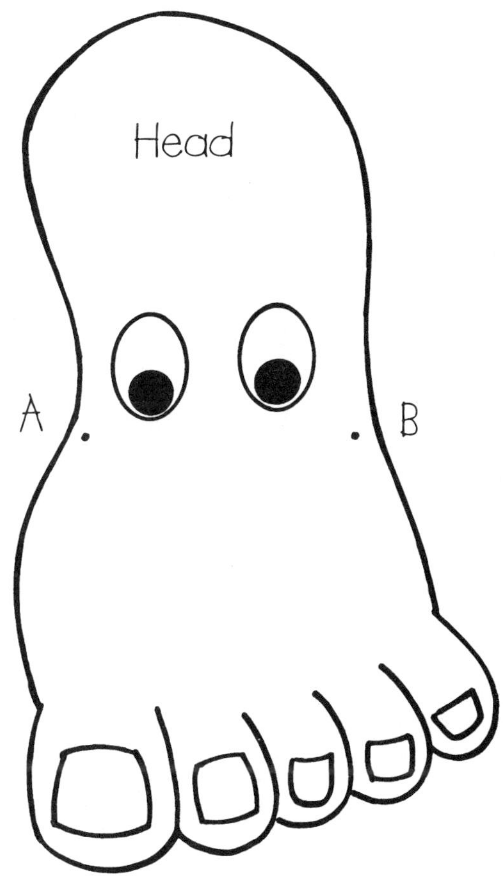

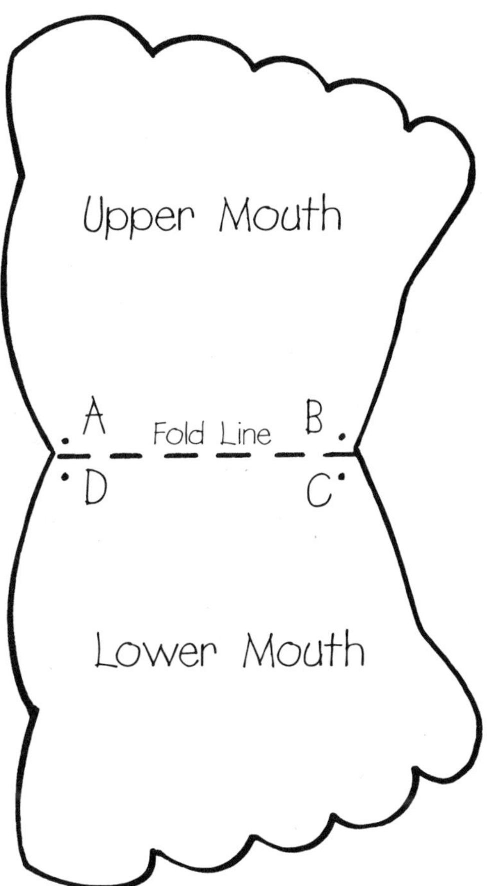

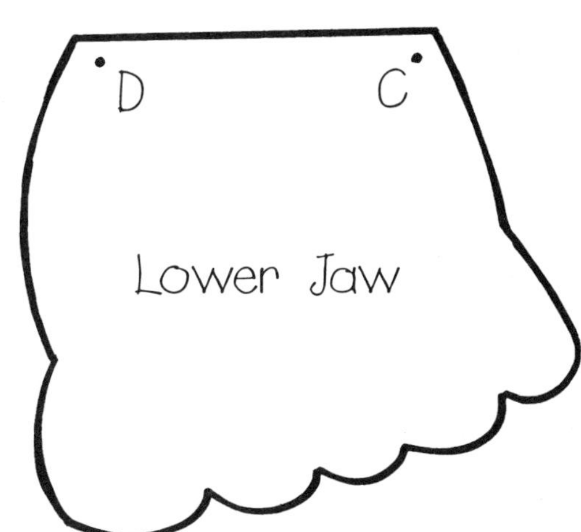

Hand Puppet (Make Two)      

1. Cut two hands from felt. Cut one set for the right hand and invert the patterns for the left hand.
2. Assemble the puppets according to the step-by-step directions.
3. Add eyes.
4. Mark knuckles and fingernails with a fabric marker.
5. Paint fingernails, if desired.

Ideas for Using a Hand Puppet

- Teach about the time the finger of God wrote on a wall (Daniel 5:1–6, 23–28).
- Let a puppet tell how Jesus healed a withered hand (Mark 3:1–5).
- Explain the reference to clean hands and a clean heart as found in James 4:8.
- Discuss using our hands to serve others (Psalm 90:17).
- Talk about the widow who gave an offering of all she had as found in Mark 12:41–44.
- Let a puppet tell about Paul's hands that worked for God (Acts 19:11–12).
- Have a puppet tell how a potter's hands shape pottery. How does God mold and shape us as referenced in Jeremiah 18:6?
- Discuss using hands to feed the needy (James 2:14–18).
- Let a hand puppet tell about the woman who touched the cloak of Jesus for healing in Matthew 9:20–22.
- Add a wound on the hand and talk about the time that Thomas believed when he saw the wounds on Jesus (John 20:24–29).
- Clap the hands together and sing a song of praise for God's handiwork (Isaiah 40:12).
- Talk about the time Jesus drew on the ground (John 8:6).

Pattern for the Hand Puppet

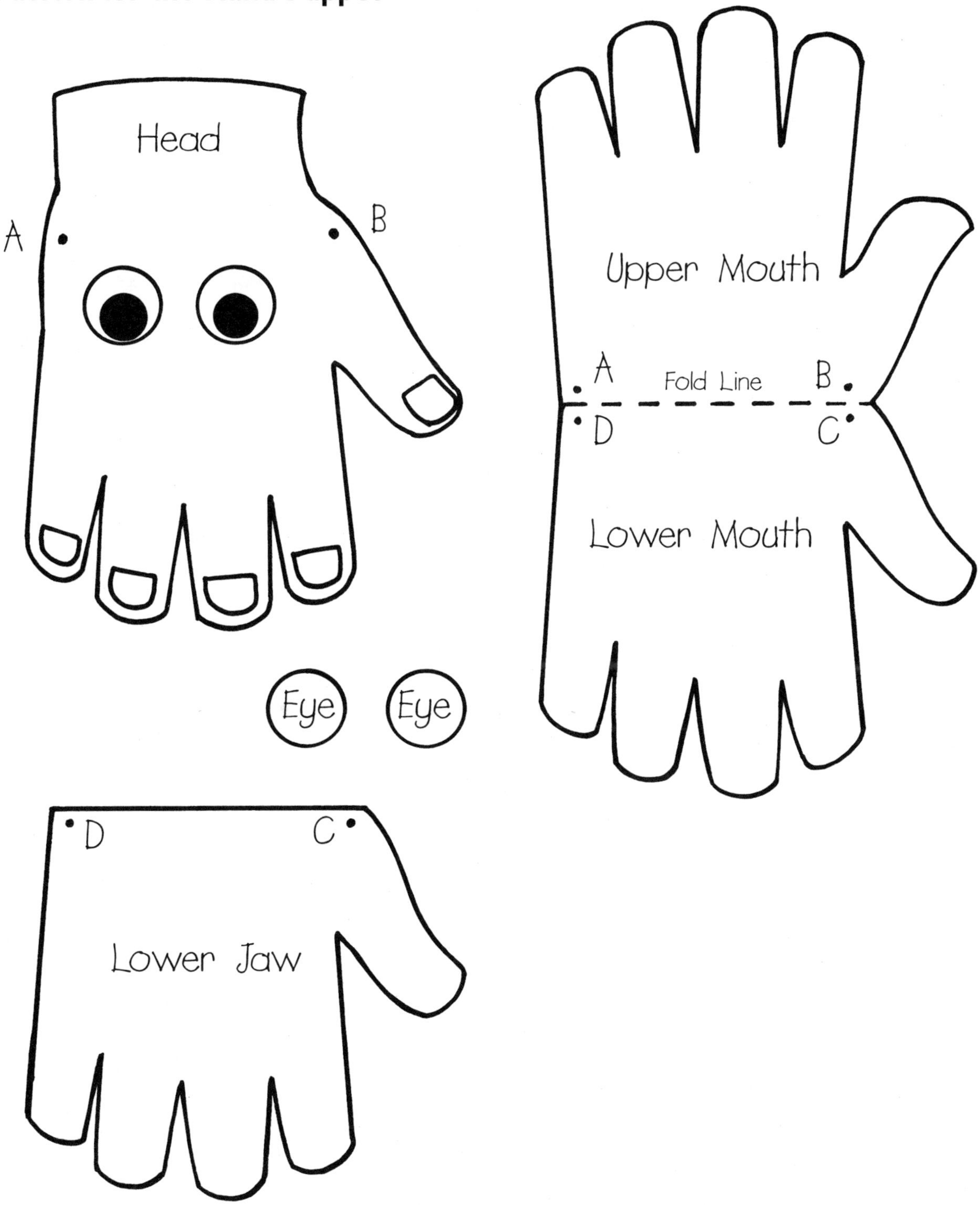

Head

A B

Eye Eye

Upper Mouth

A Fold Line B

D C

Lower Mouth

D C

Lower Jaw

Heart Puppet

1. Cut a heart from pink or red felt or cut a purple heart to symbolize courage.
2. Assemble the puppet according to the step-by-step directions.
3. Add eyes.
4. (Optional) Trim the head of the puppet with lace before assembling the puppet.

Ideas for Using a Heart Puppet

- Discuss the two greatest commandments defined by Jesus in Matthew 22:36–40. Talk about the ways to love the Lord and to love others as an outgrowth of that love.
- Let a heart puppet tell about how God sees what is in our hearts (1 Samuel 16:7).
- Teach about Proverbs 17:22 and how joy keeps us healthy.
- Tell how Mary treasured many things in her heart (Luke 2:51).
- Talk about the reward of the pure in heart (Matthew 5:8).
- Let a heart puppet lead a discussion on good things that come from a heart whose faith is focused on God (Luke 6:43–45).
- Talk about how God creates a clean heart and renews a right spirit within us (Psalm 51:10 and Ezekiel 11:19).
- Let a heart puppet ask children to tell about their love for Jesus and their faith (Romans 10:10).
- Discuss the joy of making music in our hearts (Ephesians 5:19).

Pattern for Heart Puppet

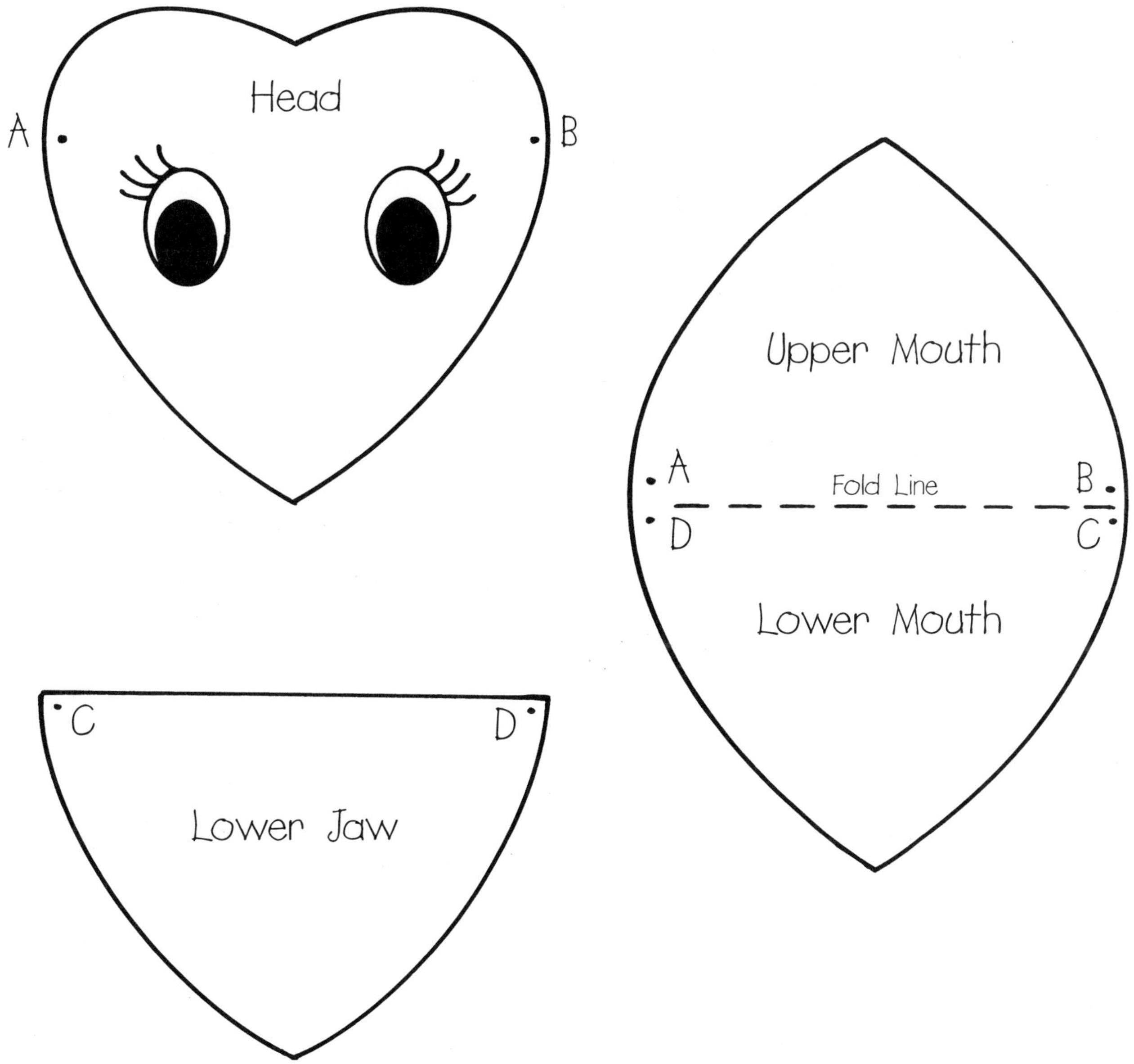

A Head B

Upper Mouth

A Fold Line B

D C

Lower Mouth

C D

Lower Jaw

Candle Puppet 

1. Cut a candle from any color of felt.
2. Assemble the puppet according to the step-by-step directions.
3. Add a yellow feather, or a piece of yellow felt, for the flame on the candle.
4. Add eyes.

Ideas for Using a Candle Puppet

- Let a candle puppet tell children that Jesus is the Light of the world (John 8:12). What do they think that means?
- Share ways for the children to let the light of their faith shine (Matthew 5:14).
- Talk about ways the light of faith can be hidden as referenced in Matthew 5:15.
- Let a candle puppet listen to ideas on how the Holy Spirit helps God's children walk in the light of faith (1 John 1:7).
- Let a candle puppet lead children in singing "Happy Birthday" to individual children and, at Christmas, to Jesus (Luke 2).
- Discuss how God's Word lights our path (Psalm 119:105).
- Talk about ways God's children can brighten the lives of others by sharing God's love.
- Teach that light was created on the first day (Genesis 1:3).
- Let a candle share how the path of the righteous is bright (Proverbs 4:18).
- Use a candle puppet to tell the parable of the 10 virgins (Matthew 25:1–13).
- Tell how candles will not be needed in the New Jerusalem (Revelation 21:23).

Pattern for Candle Puppet

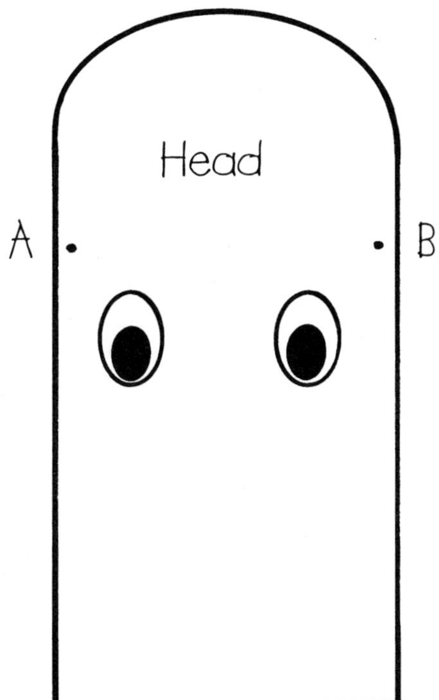

Upper Mouth

A Fold Line B

D C

Lower Mouth

C D

Lower Jaw